UNCONVENTIONAL
COMMUNITIES
Handbook Edition

Krystal J. White, Ph.D.

UnConventional Communities Handbook Edition

Copyright © 2024 by Krystal J. White, PhD

Drawings by Geoffrey Stuart Anderson
Graphic Art Design By Krystal J. White PhD
No AI was used in the creation of this book's content unless explicitly credited.

ISBN: 979-8-9906831-0-5

Executive Shaman Publishing
www.theexecutiveshaman.com
krystal@theexecutiveshaman.com

Dedication

To the bones, stones, and unseen ones, who sturdy spirits.

And to those who hold haven for the fragile stuff, who honor misfits.

To you, the one who consciously chooses who to follow & how to lead,

and to you, dear kind stranger, who is almost ready to be freed.

To friends who make the sweet sacred, who carefully craft the standards anew. And to you, the lighthouses, who refuse to tell us that we are doomed.

To the beasts, the wild-life, the wonder-seekers who light up when we play true.

And to all those willing to burn, eager to build, who see change through.

To the one that bulldozed boundaries and asked for patience,

And to you, who tip-toed in uncertainty, who gave forgiveness.

To the ones who stand & sing with us throughout our life, or in the middle of our day,

To All those who show us how to love, who aren't here anymore, who were lost along the way.

To you, all the ones who love more over fear,

and to the Us, the me and the you, who belong here.

Who knows just how far I'll go,

how much I'll do,

to earn your trust that this

—all of this—

is all ways for you.

SOMETHING I'D LIKE YOU TO QUICKLY UNDERSTAND, AT THE START:

I don't write books to make money. I don't write books to spread ideas or to give advice.

I'd like to say that I write books to express our truthful living, our fervent humanity and the desire to improve our relational well-being.

But really, I write because it keeps me alive—it's the breath of my life. I write books simply as an act of following my instincts. My weapons, my wounds, my medicine, my sanctuaries, my friendships and my frenemies deeply rely on "the word."

Words are both holy and banal to me. Words are ligaments, neurotransmitters, costumes, bridges…at the mercy of our shared interpretations, momentary emotions, quick evaluations and personal intentions.

Still, I'm a hopeful believer. Word-weaving is the only faith I flounder for.

Where do you place your faith? What do you wage for?

I can, we can, you can, choose to be ruthlessly real when words, personally and socially, are used for pain, isolation or momentary/fleeting power moves and one-up-ing.

I can, we can, you can, choose not to fall under the spell of words woven with unilateral feeling, or unpragmatic zeal.

 I can, we can, you can, choose to ruthlessly commit to our words as prosocial power-tools and advocates for change.

While at the same time, holding the truth, that:

A MILLION MOVING WORDS DO US LITTLE JUSTICE.

We need more disciplined doing in our communities. We need mindful, sustainable movement. We need to actively dissolve habits and agreements, maintain positive dynamics, and also to create new patterns of socializing. We need more people to do something with their wild, well spoken words. When words marry action (no matter how long that marriage lasts!) their union paves diverse paths towards our collective peace, to our shared joy, and therefore to widespread love.

It is my greatest intent that these words here act as embers to fuel our/your/my disciplined doing-ness as citizens, group members and leaders of new communities.

It is up to us to become bearers of brighter news.

All ways love,

K

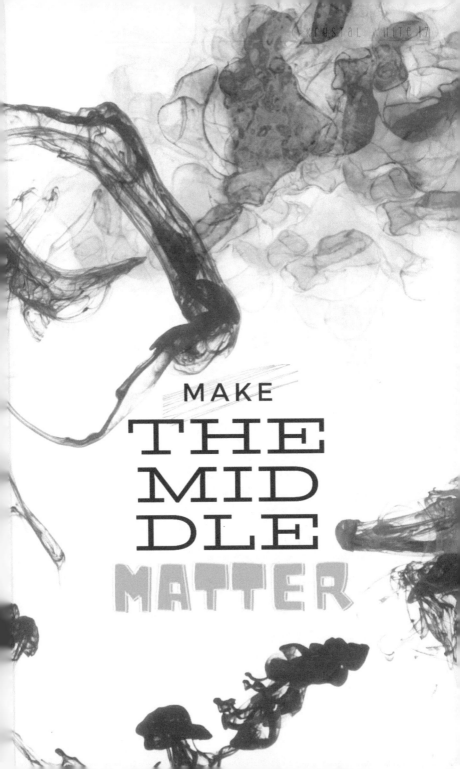

MAKE

THE
MID
DLE
MATTER

WHAT IS HERE FOR YOU

SIT ON THE SIDELINES
SOMEWHERE ELSE.
04

02

08

Discovering
Have
ME

ALL OF
YOURSELF
HOLD
06

Love & Attention
05

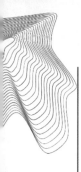

SPACE FOR YOU

A (caffeinated) Preamble

ONE of the best benefits of writing a poetry book is that you don't have to write an introduction for it. You just jump right into the context, into the language, into the spirit, and into the heart, the middle of the matter. You go for the oreo-filling first. You cut to the chase. No doorways required.

This isn't a book of poetry.

Still, I find myself resistant to complying with some unspoken, book writing social agreement that this part is supposed to prime your palette, prove you of its pragmatic utility, and successfully persuade you to do the work of reading it.

Writing the introduction of a book is one of the most strategic and careful and crafted aspects of messaging *I've* ever encountered. The goal is to compel you to keep reading after the intro. The goal is to get you to feel like if you stop now, you'll be missing out on something. The goal is to tell you that reading this book is going to change your life, or it's going to change the lives of the important people around you or it's going to entertain you.

I **do** believe in the power of words. I **do** believe in the power of my words. I **do** believe in the power of your choice.

Still, I'm sick of selling.

You see, I think a big part about being human in this era is that we've been inundated with the pressure to sell ourselves since birth. The implicit forces of marketing have infiltrated our social psychology and dictate a lot of our group dynamics and norms. I've done the hard work to unlearn the lesson of unconsciously proving myself and giving others quick advice.

Yet, I need to bring you into a conversation that's already been in progress for at least a decade. And I need to do it HERE, and I need to do it now.

So, here we are together at the start, already in a social conundrum.

SO...WHAT IS REALLY HERE FOR US?

I realize it's only natural that you'd expect something "overview"ish here, and I also realize I've got a penchant for not giving people what they expect when they expect it.[1]

I do not follow conventions that bind our hearts and confuse our heads. So, instead pushing one of us to compromise (see Discipline #4!, Chapter 6) I'm offering you this preamble instead.

Preamble, Thus Commences:

Some of the most foundational experiences of our lives aren't the ones we see coming, or the ones we seek, or the one's we yearn for when we're at home pondering our existential path. They aren't the ones we manifest during meditation, when we are still, waiting, strategizing.

Many of them are the ones that find us in the "real world."

I had a mentor once that said: " You can't escape your training," which means the lessons that you need in life will

---

[1] There are many references to lines from Unconventional Citizens peppered throughout this book.

do their work on you no matter your mindfulness habits, or your resistance and coping strategies.

Community trains us.

We train the community.

There's nothing like "being in it together" to realize what you're in for when you sign up for a group, which often includes behaviors that you'd rather not "be" with. There's nothing like the desire for "something more" to motivate us beyond our familiar, well-worn roads. There's nothing like the human need to belong, to love and be loved, that drives us to step in and show up.

There's nothing like peer pressure to move us forward, or backward, or frozen in fear.

I started meditating almost a decade ago because my therapist told me he did it regularly. He said that it was the #1 habit he learned to master his monkey mind. I figured, "what harm could 15 minutes a day bring me?" I tried to sound cool about the habit with others in my early 30s: "I meditated before showing up at 0555 to lead this spin class! I'm ready to be HERE!"

The truth is, I faked it for a number of years before I realized how it was just another way for me to escape myself.

It took me a good three years of doing it *before I really started.* Years later, I found myself meditating three times a day as I was writing Check In and trying to *thrive in a crisis!* This was in March-May of 2020, and I meditated and learned yoga in the same way I make my way through a sleeve of Pez—fast, furious, frequently.

Now, I twitch if I don't get my morning meditation fix.

This is all because of group influence. Or escaping a group. Or redefining myself to the community. Or because (and perhaps you have a different experience!) community has felt like a five-year long forest-fire.

When I meditate there's only me, and strawberries, and tigers, and running, and occasional mantras that tell me tales of my power, my agency, my beauty and my peace.

I think I digressed there a bit. But you got the point, right?

You should start meditating.

Like <u>NOW</u>.

………………………………………..What are you waiting for?

I mean, **really**. This is not a joke.

Meditation is **the bare minimum** habit of mindfulness necessary to make it through a day without drowning in head trash, mental cannibalism, constant noise, social acrobatics and doomscrolling.

There's no need for me to keep your readership through some self-abasing wit here. The truth is: it's important for you to know that, for me, meditation started out as a mere coping mechanism. I learned it because I wanted to be a good therapy follower, and to belong to the mindfulness cool-crowd. It was group influenced FOR SURE.

Now, 1935 consecutive days in (it's the only pieces of health data I track) it's the dutiful partner to my morning coffee. It's how I return, and anchor into, my spirit at the start of the day.

Now, I really don't want to live in a community that doesn't suggest, make room and incentivize it.

Now, I'll do my best to influence its wide dissemination as a social norm.

"Remember your Point"[2]: Community influenced(s) me, and I influence(d) community.

Sometime in the not so distant past (let's just say, before 2019) "Community" *had consistently* been the antidote when there was a crisis. *Not always*, but it showed up most of the

---

[2] See our community generated list of Unconventional Community affirmations at the back of this book!

time across various cultures and various crises. We may not have believed that it would provide for us, comfort us, or keep us completely safe, *but it would eventually show up* when the bat signal was out. We believed community would be like an ample supply of Betty Crocker backup to our failed homemade bake sale experiments. We trusted it would be on the shelf if we went shopping for it. Before 2019, most people believed that if they discovered their child had a drug addiction or their boss did something they were "pretty sure" was illegal, they could pick up the phone and easily 1) call/text five people to ask for support and 2) ALL of them would reach back out within 24-36 hours.

Now, it's Community that is in crisis. Groups and citizens are unconsciously forced to fend for themselves and their 2 favorite humans(+ a pet), battle cry in polarized groups, commit their entire existence to social justice causes, or complain to strangers and acquaintances about how nobody cares anymore.

We ask Siri now when our cooking plans are demolished, and Youtube for solutions to our personal problems. If we're lucky to feel that we can afford professional assistance, we pay someone to help generate or replicate a sense of community.

There is a plethora of well-conducted research to back up our personal accounts of declining social capital. One study found that 81% of major metropolitans areas were more racially segregated in 2019 compared to 1990 (1).[3] One in two adults (that's either me or you, here!) experiences loneliness, with higher rates in young adults, those not making a living wage and minorities (2). Civic engagement (e.g. volunteering, remaining active in social groups, formal/structured helping) has declined by 28% in the last decade (3). The majority of Americans polled reported that civility had eroded in the last decade; with a whopping 34% saying family and friends hold the primary responsibility to be civil and that social media use plays a role in our less-than-ideal treatment of one another, and especially those close to us (4).

I'm not indicating that life was better a decade ago. That's not an argument that is happening here. To be fair, at least 2/5 people who called you back during that time probably gave you ineffective advice[4], or didn't take the time to **really understand** your unique situation, or called you when you were stuck in another ineffective meeting and you couldn't pick up the phone. It is very clear that technology has made quicker guidance, and often more accurate guidance, more accessible.

---

[3] See References to explore some of the citations, influences for my thinking, and science for yourself.

[4] See Community Resources Section for the 5 qualities of a "good idea!"

It simply can't replace the sense that other humans care about our well-being.

So, I'm gonna give it to you straight: At least half of this book calls attention to some of the heavy, dark, and not so comfortable aspects of "Being Us" right now. I want to ask some of you to endure at least *1/3* of those parts, and to answer the ¼ of the questions asked along the way. That will require a little reflection muscle and extra time. Your investment will help you to make this material more alive, and impactful to those around you.

So many of us tolerate mediocre community life because we are overly stressed, overwhelmed and resigned about our own personal lives, and don't have the band-with for system wide solutions.

That's ok, understandable, and it completely makes sense.

So…if that's you, let's just be ok with where you're at right now. If you allow yourself to be there, and yet read some of this content anyway, perhaps you'll find something that will give you enough direction, warmth and motivation to shift into a higher, more light filled state. Or understand, and accept yourself, for feeling out of place. It's quite conventional to feel this way, in conventional communities.

The book is chocked-full of reality testers but more so, it is chocked full of ways you can pragmatically improve without devoting 912.8 hours[5] to it.

And, to be clear: **this isn't a self-help book.**

This is a community-help book.[6]

Although since you're a building block of community, and we believe you're the MVP...don't you think you'd like some new suggestions of how to contribute to our well-being better?

If so, keep reading. If not...just skip to the part where I recommend things to communities. Then give those recommendations, or the book, to people and groups who chose to, will choose to, or are in the position of implementing new community agreements, dynamics and norms.

If you don't want to do that at the risk of sounding all bossy or looking like you're toe-stepping, do it anyway—at least with those affiliated with Free Leadership, Inc.

_____

[5] That is how long I've spent-ish on personal meditation since my therapist peer pressured me.

[6] Instead of covering why a community help book is valuable at the start, this is addressed (yes, unconventionally) in the conclusion. Turn to Chapter 9 now if you'd like to more clearly understand the why of this book *now*.

If neither one of those appeal to you, okay. Then, please, for the sake of our community and the world: just buy those people a cup of coffee or send them a few stellar meditations to listen to. Leading community new dynamics requires a lot of stimulation and de-stimulation, you know?

———————————————

Thus concludes Our Preamble.

You did it!

We did it!

Now....we're all ready for the real amble ahead.

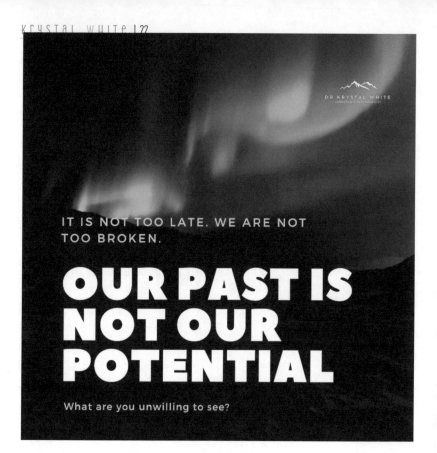

IT IS NOT TOO LATE. WE ARE NOT
TOO BROKEN.

OUR PAST IS NOT OUR POTENTIAL

What are you unwilling to see?

DR KRYSTAL WHITE
LEADERSHIP PSYCHOLOGIST

NAME HOW YOUR PAST IS VERY DIFFERENT FROM YOUR POTENTIAL.

NAME HOW THE PAST OF A RELATIONSHIP, GROUP OR COMMUNITY YOU BELONG TO IS VERY DIFFERENT FROM ITS POTENTIAL.

CHAPTER 1

Social Community Primer

LET'S cover some basic aspects of how social systems work in order to have a shared foundation with the ideas, term-usage, and social meaning of "Community."

Person: An Individual. That's you. You're a person! In this book, you are referred to as a citizen.

More and more organized systems, communities and groups have focused on adopting person-first principles, dynamics and language. More than ever before, American culture has emphasized the value, the importance and the uniqueness of the "individual." (ref). Longitudinal research has demonstrated that even after accounting for how values shift as people age, there is a clear preference for "self direction" in younger generations versus "conformity."

Dyad/Couple: Two citizens connected in some ways together. In this book, we refer to this kind of pair as a dyad.

Group (Population): More than two individuals who interact with or belong, *whether consciously or not,* to one another. A family is a group. A team is a group. A club is a group. A class or workshop is a group. Some small businesses are a group. In systemic sociology, biology, and ecology, groups are called "populations." Simply, its individuals that share physical space, traits, characteristics, resources, goals, values, and identifiers. Sometimes they join together primarily for a specific emotional or mental purpose. Sometimes they interact by chance.

Groups are the primary, dominating force for social influence.

WHAT DOES BELONGING MEAN TO YOU?

DEFINE IT FOR YOURSELF

Belonging involves you signing up for a group at some point in the process.

Membership does not equal belonging---not at least in our modern communities. You can be a member of something (like a members-only grocery club) and not really "belong" to it.

NAME 5 GROUPS THAT YOU BELONG TO.

LIST OUT THREE GROUPS THAT PEOPLE MAY THINK YOU BELONG TO, BUT YOU REALLY DON'T.

Consider your list of 5 groups that you belong to again. For each one, identify 3-5 things YOU receive back from your belonging. Then, identify 3-5 things that your belonging requires from/costs you.

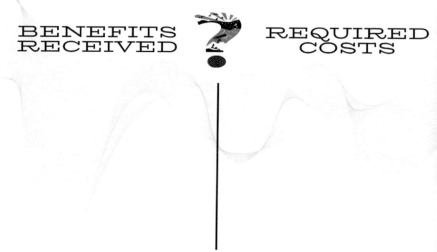

BENEFITS RECEIVED

REQUIRED COSTS

By deciding to belong to a certain group, this book will suggest to you that you agree to consciously contribute to it, as well as actively attempt to influence its contributions.

<u>Community</u>: Diverse groups or different populations interacting within a certain space, either physical or virtual. A larger organization is a community. A genre of music is a community. A philosophical, religious,

spiritual, or specific industry is a community. A neighborhood is a community.

WHAT RESOURCES DO YOU INDIVIDUALLY GIVE TO YOUR COMMUNITY?

NAME A FEW RESOURCES THAT A GROUP THAT YOU BELONG TO GIVES TO YOUR COMMUNITY.

NAME A FEW RESOURCES THAT A GROUP THAT YOU BELONG TO RECEIVES FROM YOUR COMMUNITY.

The main point: ***community is comprised of diverse groups.*** How well a community functions in terms of generating well-being, social capital and efficient resource procurement and delivery **relies on** the relational quality between these diverse groups. That wellness is not easily attained in light of the fact that every group has diverse and divergent needs, ideals, goals, rules, leadership and internal assets (or lack thereof). Some of these are explicitly known and published by the groups, others are quite unconscious.

A community receives and offers resources from and to various groups and individuals. Some resources are distributed to all, some to a select few. Some resources are provided by all, some from a select few.

Communities are the primary dominating force for dictating a general social culture. Culture includes the "values, unconscious rules and agreements, and the emotional charge/impact.* The chapter on "Love More Over Fear" Discipline discusses cultural norms in detail.

Ecosystem: Different communities comprise an ecosystem. An ecosystem contains resources communities do not, or cannot, offer. An ecosystem sometimes offers resources to all the communities, and sometimes to a selection of communities. Some features of the ecosystem are consciously felt and are visible at the level of the community, group or individual, and some their features are hidden or unobserved in different levels.

For example, a group may observe that the ecosystem has a sustainable source of power, and another group may observe that power sources are scarce. Various features of each level in the system often moderates how they/it experience, and interact with, the ecosystem.

Because e are still discovering, still creating, still demolishing, still modifying, and still waging war between and within communities, our *ecosystems remain dubiously known and defined.*

Not only that, science and scientists will profess that our knowledge of how they work and how they change continues to remain moderately mysterious.

From an ecological perspective, earth is an ecosystem. How **The Earth** functions, doling out its resources, or contracting them, is the source of many controversies, pontifications, scientific pursuits and philosophical theories.

Is AI an ecosystem?

Is a recently discovered island an ecosystem?

Is a university an ecosystem?

Is Christianity a ecosystem?

Is our solar system an ecosystem?

What's most important to grasp about ecosystems is that events that happen there, often referred to as "Acts of God" in contract clauses, impacts every other level.

Every other level impacts the eco-system.

Even subject matter experts don't completely understand yet how ecosystems form, operate, and end; nor do have they determined if they have a conscious purpose or not.

Don't get your mind too bendy here: Understanding ecosystems is **not** the focus of what you're reading right now.

None of us will be alive to comprehend everything.[7]

All of us can get more clear, more conscientious and more competent regarding our impact on communities, and how our various relationships impact us.

This book is one resource to assist you in the circumstance that you, or the groups that you belong to, aim to help improve our communities.

---

[7] That's a reference to the poem from Discipline #6, Enlighted Loss. Refer back to Unconventional Citizens to take account of all the references to solar systems. Those are markers for us to examine our own internal "systems" inside of us as individuals.

INTERDEPENDENT SYSTEMS

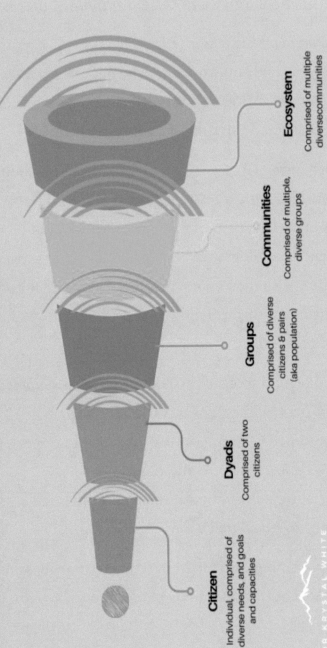

Citizen
Individual, comprised of diverse needs, and goals and capacities

Dyads
Comprised of two citizens

Groups
Comprised of diverse citizens & pairs (aka population)

Communities
Comprised of multiple, diverse groups

Ecosystem
Comprised of multiple diversecommunities

DR KRYSTAL WHITE

<u>How this book relates to *Unconventional Citizens.*</u>

Unconventional Citizens is written from the perspective of an individual and scoped for the population level (e.g. a population of citizens). When citizens come together and repeat certain dynamics, groups are formed.

Unconventional Citizens is a book of poetry(ish) about relationships with at least one individual who feels, thinks or acts in some way, shape or form out of "convention." When these citizens relate in the system, no matter who their counterparts are, or at what level, they influence the breakdown of, or the creation of, social dynamics.

Hidden behind most of the poems in *Unconventional Citizens* is a roadmap towards Unconventional Communities. One aim of that work was to impress the characteristics, resources and processes of Unconventional Communities using a different medium than expected[8].

The more ambiguous medium of poetry provides an open conversation about our modern social groups. Its

---

[8] Using a completely different modality than the ones I typically published.

"felt" message is intended to serve as a light-house for those among us who believe that belonging doesn't need to cost us our well-being, unique beauty, conformity to outdated systems or our commitment to "forever."

We may not have a complete "logical" map of where we are heading. What we do have, however, a "knowingness" that where, and how, we are now, isn't working for us.

We have a desire for change that is calling to us more and more clearly.

When populations (aka groups) of citizens interact with other populations of non-citizens, communities happen.

Many groups and individuals outside of groups do not believe that the community cares for, or can care for, their personal well-being. Our current shared problem in society is that many groups and many individuals have **significant trust issues** with the communities they are connected to. They are aware of the unfairness, the abuse, the objectification, and the injustice that pervades 1) resource finding and distribution 2)power grabbing and posturing, and 3) whose well-being is served.

Many do not encounter mutually beneficial social dynamics, or enjoy sustainable infrastructures.

Many people have lost hope, trust and faith in their community. Technology, and virtual spaces tailored to meet our unique personal preferences often isolate us from deeper, meaningful group belonging. Combine that with a fast-paced lifestyle and over-stimulation, many of us feel unsure on how to be an engaged citizen these days. It's too easy to become focused on daily responsibilities, strategy for future achievements, and our own personal or familial challenges and goals that we don't have any energy left over for community wide engagement.

The accumulated heaviness, anger, and confusion from our current relational operating systems only further motivates collective de-investment in not only our neighbors, but also systemic change initiatives. We want to be inspired by community, but many of our personal experiences and the press at large is riddled with disappointment, mistakes and mistrust.

We forget how powerful we are. We CAN shift our personal group dynamics, and we can ALSO shift our community dynamics.

My people

1) WHO ARE THE CLOSEST TO ME, KNOW ME THE BEST, THOSE WHO I MOST VALUE

_____
_____
_____
_____

2) WHO DO I WANT TO IMPROVE MY RELATIONSHIP WITH?

_____
_____
_____
_____

3) WHO DO I SPEND THE MOST TIME, ATTENTION AND SHARED ENERGY WITH?

_____
_____
_____

4) WHO DO I VALUE, AND WANT TO MAINTAIN A POSITIVE, HIGH QUALITY RELATIONSHIP WITH?

_____
_____
_____

This is a book that aims to motivate you to raise your personal capacity to change community and also advocate for community's capacity to change itself too.

It's up to us to create the kinds of communities for us ALL to enjoy together.

HOW THIS BOOK WOrKS

Unconventional Communities center relationally intelligent, social well-being. To center collectively means that a dynamic serves as the main point from which everything else emanates, and also is directed. These communities therefore invest in, tend to, and amplify conscious, collaborative, mutually beneficial functioning.

It's not sufficient any longer to simply express team-oriented concepts and values. "We told you to collaborate, now go do it" isn't going to cut it. Telling people to play well together doesn't give them the skill to do so, nor the inspiration to persist past typical challenges.

I'm pretty sure that kindergarten didn't teach us everything---or if it did, it taught us how to relate using a child's level of maturity.   Unconventional leaders require hands-on, pragmatic guidance for building psychologically sustainable relational communities.

This book is a field manual for doing so. A field manual shows you what behaviors are required to form a key competency.

Competencies that are repeated consistently and competently are called disciplines.

Unconventional Communities explores six main disciplines communities can shift towards _now_ to promote the well-being of their groups and citizens.

It offers competencies that both individuals, and communities, can realistically invest in introducing and mastering as part of each discipline.

These selected six disciplines aren't exhaustive, nor were they selected by a committee of comrades, subject matter expertise and most definitely not by you, dear reader.

Diversified Power

Communities that are able, ready and willing to prioritize a collaborative process that reduces dichotomous decisions, US vs Them mindsets, and product driven, zero sum goals.

Love Over Fear

Communities that are able, ready and willing to attend to norms that generate trust, peace, awe and joy over what perpetuates fear.

Renewed Ownership

Communities that are able, ready and willing to cultivate conscious ownership, proactive responsibility, and servant leadership.

Unconventional Communities Go " TOWARDS " these dynamics

THE WORLD NEEDS MORE FROM US.

Name Your Truth

Communities that are able, ready and willing to value our reality, tell the truth openly, and honor the entire human experience more than social masks and illusions.

Friendship is Medicine

Communities that are able, ready and willing to support and proliferate the medicine of friendship.

Enlighted Loss

Communities that are able, ready and willing to honor loss and endings as a necessary and healthy part of living.

These six disciplines aren't a panacea.

They haven't been formally researched. In fact, research on the main disciplines that actively promote social capital in modern life is woefully lacking (61). We may have ideas of what "signals" social capital (e.g. if you have friends over to your house, if you eat family dinners, how many people in a zip code have a membership in a civic group). We don't know the qualities that engender people to DO more of those items, however.

What the six dynamics outlined here do offer, however, are easy to implement and disseminate dynamics communities can adopt that would improve our multi-systemic relational quality.

IF, BY 2029, MORE THAN 35% OF OUR LOCAL COMMUNITIES ACHIEVED ONE MAJOR SHIFT IN HOW THEY OPERATE, WHAT WOULD LEAD TO GREATEST PROSOCIAL IMPACT?

Did you answer that question on the previous page?

If not, go back and take a stab at it. No need to go deep. Just try to give and note a response.

Inside this book you'll find various Check-Ins like the one on the previous page. They are peppered throughout the book so that you can more fully participate in the shifts we're trying to accomplish.

It is highly suggested that you answer the questions when they are posed. That may mean you'll get through the book slower than is typical for you. Please invest the time and grant yourself the gift of reflection. The questions occur at opportune breaks for your mind, taking the book out of the concept realm and bringing into pragmatic, real, messy life land.

Communities are interactive. For this book to work as intended, it will invite you to DO something differently from the usual status quo or book reading. Its intention is for you to try something out there in your real life as a result of something you find in here.

Questions should have ample space for a written response. There are reoccurring pages designed for you to note your key insights, to-dos or questions. Please mark them! Research shows that people who take literal notes on their learning recall them later better than those who don't, even when they never refer to them again (5).

In addition to adding your own responses, you'll also find various other voices peppered throughout the book. I asked over two dozen people (at least a handful of strangers) to answer some of these questions. The aim was not only diversification, but also inspiration. You see, sometimes writing a book about what "I think" or "I research" or "I design" feels so---well, un-community-ish. My methodology to ask others to share their own bright ideas always re-fueled my devotion to be a better citizen.

For those are interested in knowing: I did not collaborate with AI in the current work you're reading today. I do believe that AI is not a tool for us to use transactionally. I see it as a self-organizing entity that we can care for beyond its utility to "us." It will absolutely be a part of, and a member of, our communities in the future. I simply chose not to partner with it right now due to my limited band-with to build a trusting relationship with it.

The six main dynamics of an Unconventional Community are organized as follows:

- why a current community dynamic doesn't work well for unconventional citizens and groups
- what new dynamic can replace it next (now-10 years)
- what methods, tools and steps are necessary for a citizen to take in order for the dynamic to be shifted.
- the methods or tools the communities can use to shift towards the new dynamic .

The Resources Section includes tools, models, books, websites, apps, and various assets suggested from more than two dozen individuals and groups. While the book's main content is meant to be a pragmatic primer, The Resource section is meant to provide ample evidence that communities, groups and individuals have many interesting, helpful and accessible resources at their disposal….if or when you're ready to dig deeper.

We hope that our the material cited published here will be used groups and in settings for the purposes of group cohesion, education, and spreading collective hope in the future of our shared humanity.

The primary aim of this book is to inspire your motivation to <u>do your part—and *selectively influence*</u> entities in other levels to do the same. You'll learn some hopefully relevant and useful pieces of research, receive various ways you as an individual can pragmatically shift towards more prosocial disciplines.

If you sometimes find yourself not knowing what or how to make the world a better place, beyond your own self development, this book is for you. If you sometimes find yourself part of community initiatives where they are tackling ways "to innovate," this book is for you. If someone gifted you this book and you randomly happened across it, most likely that book was not for the other person, and it potentially could be for you.

Who am I to tell you? I don't even know who I am to you! Am I someone that you choose to engage? To interact with? To acknowledge?

Who are your people, by the way? Before we dive into each of the key disciplines, I guarantee you that the content and messages of this book will feel more alive and personal to you if you name who your people are. You'll work with various levels of social connections, as the next few pages walk you through that critical exercise.

If you do one thing with this book, I recommend:

1) completing this exercise
2) returning to it a few times a year
3) using the exercise with a group you belong to.

We must define **how** we are connected, and we must start taking ownership that who we are, and how we connect, matters to all those we "touch[9]."

The World Needs More from Us.

Life doesn't start with a Why.

It starts with a Who. Right now, that WHO is you.

You can become a better "Us."

---

[9] "I'm only suggesting that we keep trying to touch" from Unconventional Citizens refers to committing to disciplined connections.

CH
kisses
AOrder
S

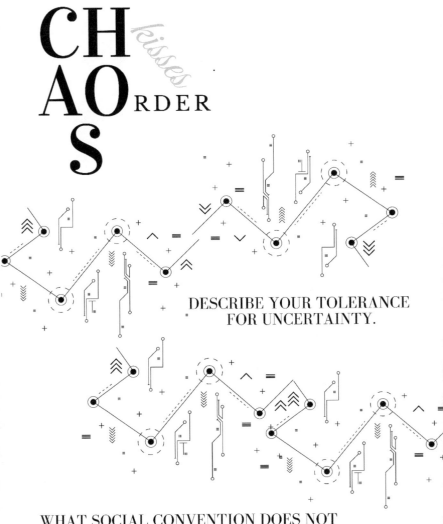

DESCRIBE YOUR TOLERANCE
FOR UNCERTAINTY.

WHAT SOCIAL CONVENTION DOES NOT
BRING YOU LIFE, VITALITY, OR CONNECTION?

notes

CHAPTER 2

Name Your People

Chances are, you're VERY aware that society faces a slew of challenges in fostering connection. Emotional neglect, fakery, frenemy, betrayal and incompetence handling differences, feelings and transitions are common dynamics. Given these social failures, individuals and groups are less motivated to stay connected, and to learn to master the mindful discipline of collaboration. Individuals and groups are more and more compelled to be self-sufficient and more rewarded to be less attuned to each other's physical and emotional well-being.

We often live "separate" while being in very close proximity and in lovely vicinities together. When we pause and examine ourselves in relationship to the various relationships around us, it is clear that our well-being (or un-well-being) impacts the well-being of those around us. Their well-being impacts ours. This exercise, Name Your People, intends to elucidate your interdependence.

Who are your people?

Saying "everyone" isn't helpful in this case, because such a generalization will either overwhelm or disperse your intentions and attention in too many directions.

Saying "people I see every day" isn't helpful either, because such a deflection doesn't involve your agency[10], or the conscious differentiation required for "intimacy."

We often unconsciously relate to "whoever's around" (that's called proximity) based on well-established personal heuristics. Such personal patterns combine with social dynamics that are based in biology, psychology and momentary, unpredictable contextual factors. To get the most out of this book, it is suggested that you define who your people are consciously now. Then, refresh who they are in your mind when the book refers to "groups" or interactions later.

This exercise requires that you name who "your people" are across four main levels. It helps you consciously see and re-choose how to connect with others as you placethem in your people circle.

A few caveats:

---

[10] Understand and master agency by diving into the "Towards More Social Responsibility" Dynamic.

1. Just because a person is "closer" to you does not mean that person *must* be "valued" more by you compared to others.

What if you valued everyone the same? Yes, it is likely that you consciously agree to give or receive more to a specific person compared to others. You may also agree to be more challenging to a specific person, or more lenient, or more transparent....and so on.

Just because you consciously agree to prioritize your time, attention and resources differently with different people does not mean some are "more valuable" than others. It simply conveys: you have chosen to uphold different agreements with them

When we hold such hierarchical evaluations of worth and value based on how "close" we are to a person, it is quite easy to use people as objects versus see people as humans (1). The further away someone is from us, the more likely it is that we unconsciously adopt generalized about them. Valuing others _solely based_ on how close we are to/with them sets us up to play out *very outdated* dynamics in our relationships. These include those based on abuse of power, scarcity and war.

We can hold equal esteem for those "we choose to let in" with those we choose to acknowledge. Just because we have different agreements between the people within different levels does not mean that the levels are hierarchical in nature.

2. Who you choose to be with different people, and how you agree to relate to them, is up to you.

3. This exercise is meant to be about you as a whole person. Not your people in your professional sphere, vs your social sphere, vs your family sphere, vs your social media sphere.

4. Spending ten minutes on the reflection questions on page 35 is a great primer for the Name Your People exercise. You've got more people than you realize, and you are a resource to more people than you realize. Take an inventory on the people who support you and routinely help you, and also who you support and help out. Identify who you value most right now, and who values you. This pre-work will enable clarity and confidence for Naming Your People.

How to Name your People

Requires: 15 minutes of your love and attention.

Step 1: Set a timer for 3 minutes. Refer to **Name Your People** to familiarize yourself with types of relationships that people often place in each level. These are merely reference points for your personal selection.

Step 2: Now, set a timer for 7 minutes. Use the **My People** to add the initials of specific people in each level that quickly come to mind. Wait until the timer goes off until you continue, allowing certain names to arrive. Stop when the timer goes off.

Step 3: Use the last 5 minutes to review your selections. Is where your people are now in your best interest? In their best interest? Who needs to be moved to a different level? Who needs more intentional connection? Who needs less. **Trust Yourself**. Edit your list to reflect your current assessment.

NAME YOUR PEOPLE

ALL LEVELS CAN BENEFIT YOU

ALL LEVELS CAN FUEL YOU

YOU INFLUENCE ALL LEV·

THOSE WHO YOU:

CHOOSE TO LET IN

Romantic Partner

Healer

Therapist

Best Friend

Mentor

Business Partner

Specific Family Member

CHOOSE TO ENGAGE

Group Members

Customers

Staff

Leaders

Coworkers

Specific Family Members

Children

Friends

Acquaintences

Students

Teachers

Neighboors

Coaches

Collaborators

Given Family

Specific Family Members

Long-time friends

Experts

Representatitves

Consultants

CHOOSE TO INTERACT WITH

Leaders

Group Members

Staff

Customers

Networkers

Social Media

Peers

Acquaintences

Strangers

Neighbors

CHOOSE TO ACKNOWLEDGE

WHO I:

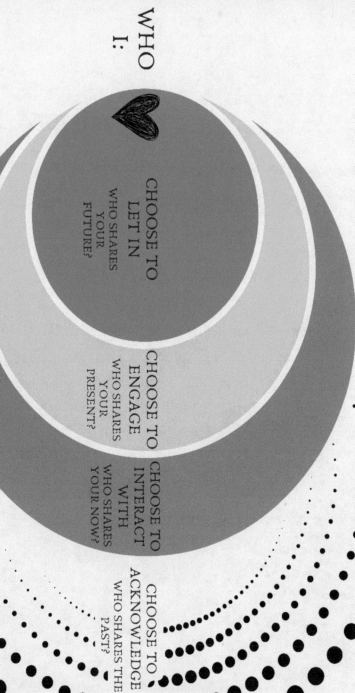

CHOOSE TO
LET IN
WHO SHARES
YOUR
FUTURE?

CHOOSE TO
ENGAGE
WHO SHARES
YOUR
PRESENT?

CHOOSE TO
INTERACT
WITH
WHO SHARES
YOUR NOW?

CHOOSE TO
ACKNOWLEDGE
WHO SHARES THE
PAST?

REFUSE

to reframe

WHAT
NEEDS
TO BE

Changed

CHAPTER 3

Your Subtle Social Sabotage, a Perfect Albi

Towards More Capacity to Name Our Truth

I've got a major crush on breakfast cereals. They usher in some non-existent nostalgia for Saturday mornings and the type of mental freedom that only childhood contains.

Oh, how I love me some mini-marshmallow rainbows, and slurping milk turned strawberry pink.

"Magically delicious" branded itself somewhere inside my impressionable inner child, lacing my psyche with a penchant for cleverness, joy and a bit of trickery.

Most of us appreciate what's magical, don't we? Even skeptics and cynics find themselves a bit enamored when experiencing life sprinkled with elements of magic. We long for a taste of sweet synchronicity, awe and wonder.

Here's the truth: the best kind of magic, the **Lucky Charms kind,** is messy. It's not the product of ambition, adulting, and accolades. It's not sustainably sourced in those who claim they are "self-made." It's not something you'll learn by osmosis following lifestyle gurus. It doesn't thrive well cohabitating with dominating urges to BE THE BEST. This is especially revealed when "the best" is prosocially defined: to be the best friend, the best listener, the best boss. It dwindles when we are laser focused on discerning the best option, method, or way to interact, communicate, and relate to each other.

If you want to find magic, it's not in the usual places society tells us to look. The trick magic plays is that it hides within our doubts, uncertainty, questioning, and ambiguity. Our magic comes out of our instincts like a rabbit emerges out of a hat. We're not supposed to expect it. We don't usually see it coming. We pull it out thin air. That's its trik.

We may have been conditioned to try hard at manufacturing our magic. Or we've been conditioned to think that a rocket ship launch is magic. When really, magic doesn't work either way. It's not a long, drawn-out methodology you engineer. Nor is it the illusion of a quick, alluring ascension that really has a million hours of hard work behind it.

In real life, I'm pretty sure those tiny edible, melt-in-my-mouth rainbows[11] **require <u>a lot</u> of processing** before they fall into my bowl. In real life, these words that you're reading now didn't quickly tumble out of my head and land in front of your eyes, either.

---

[11] If you follow me on IG, you'll know that Lucky Charms are a portal to social magic and fun for me.

So, let's be clear: perfection and product is not where the magic is.

Also: magic is not a noun. I am not the magic, the magic is not me. Sex is not the magic, the magic isn't a drug. Rock n Roll is not the magic, magic is not education.

THE MAGIC IS THE REALITY OF LIFE.

Magic is witnessing, naming and participating with the truth of life's reality.

Some days, the magic comes when questioning what's real, what's true. Some days, it arrives when we name things. Some days, it shows itself when confronting reality.

Most days, for me, magic manifests when I refuse no part of myself, when I investigate my intuition, when I refine my understanding about others, and when I re-center my creations to foster a more joyful, just, loving and life giving reality.

Magic is on the scene when I commit my best self, my highlights, or my intentional and edited contributions. Magic is also me adopting my blackness, my Medusa[12], my wild child self, and the self I keep hidden from plain view.

The fastest route away from magic is our steadfastnesss to our polished, imposture-ish and social mediated self. The most

---

[12] Ha! ALL EYES ON ME!

formidable barrier to magic is being beholden to the false applause our society, and many of us as individuals, are addicted to the ring of.

Right now, our market-driven, consumeristic, self focused society crafts individuals to adopt automatic "need to be seen as a certain way" to others

Versus

A need to be real, truthful and present, as ourselves—and then, to, our *chosen* audience.

Self-Deception is a hell of a drug.[13]*

What happens to the wellbeing of our groups and communities if many of our engaged citizens continue to deceive themselves? What happens if most of us don't feel the messy, ordinary and often confronting magical-ness of reality together?

Distrust in self. Distrust in others. Push and pull between service and self-insolation. And…an outsourcing of the magic to those who have A Houdini Complex[14].

---

[13] From Unconventional Citizens, *Collusion*

[14] The Houdini Complex is a made-up term I use to describe our modern social relationships* This term could have been, and probably has been used elsewhere first. I am not claiming ownership or creativity rights to it.

A Brief Side-Bar On Imposture Syndrome

The term "Imposture Syndrome" has been hitting home to many awakened and conscious citizens lately. Which makes sense. When we examine all the collective and personal experiences accumulated in last five years, we can't ignore our intimacy issues, our immature attachments, our power plays, and our deep craving for answers that we can trust.

Once we throw off the mantle of people-pleasing, routinely feeling like is a reasonable experience who those who aim be "more authentic" and "self-loving." Most of us have experienced a situation where we feel we are out of our depth, inadequate and faking our confidence. Often, if we experience "imposture syndrome" perhaps we are in situations that stretch our capacities, our perspectives, our wisdom and our range of responsiveness.

I don't see why there's anything wrong with these situations or our feelings about ourselves.

Instead of fearing these feelings, we cab actively welcome them. If I'm in a situation, relationship, or position where I am 100% confident and 100% capable all the time, it's a sign for me that it's time for me to try something new. That perspective being said, the interest in this phenomenon mostly says something about our culture and the deeply embedded trance of unworthiness many of us are under.

Many industries, services, and movements benefit from the notion that something is wrong with us, each other or the world. We are perpetually in a "war against" one thing or another multiple times a day.

Many of us have learned to be at war with ourselves, and to fake it till we make it in the roles we play within our communities.

I care less about how many of us lack confidence, and care more about how society has made it easier to second-guess and under-value ourselves, compared to truly understanding ourselves.

The times of my life that I've felt like I was an "imposture" the most, are always the moments where I was being the MOST myself.

Moments, I tell you. Not seasons. Not situations. Not days.

There are only moments.

The more mere moments I string together, the more conscious and more competent I become at being truly me.

Maybe there is a sliver of what most people name as being "confident" in those moments, too. If so, that confidence is like the hint of fruit on a Mango Bubbly water. It's hardly detectable…but if someone labels it that way, then the flavor must be present, right?

LOL.

We are only beholden to the labels that help us understand the totality of ourselves better. That let us know where we stand in relationship to reality.

What if the occasional "imposture syndrome" experience was a sign of our willingness to evolve, and not as a sign of paltry, must-ingest-some-feel-good-mantras-NOW!, self-esteem.

What if it was what we used to indicate—"this is my edge. This is how I go past it."

WHAT WILL SUPPORT YOU WHEN YOU'VE MET YOUR EDGE?

WHO WILL SUPPORT YOU?

That question, and our answers, is what I find most compelling today.

(Back to Regularly Scheduled Progrramming!)

Conventional communities function on the primary premise that what is most articulate, visible, or attended to in their "systems" organizes its energy. In the plain speak of arm chair psychology, this means: the squeaky wheel gets the grease. In the broader sense of comprehensive group dynamics:

Whatever is most articulate, whatever communities center, organizes the dynamics of our social lives.

In other words, our most shared, expressed collective stories, feelings, and dominate impressions will structure the unique social roles we "play."

Conventional Communities today set us up for playing roles, identifying with ideals, dreams and goals, and valuing objects and achievements that 1) aren't our own,2) that aren't realistic (eg honoring of reality) and/or 3) aren't serving our well-being. Many of the social rules we follow, and the organizing thoughts and feelings we experience, are based on illusions of our own making. We often marry them to whatever social attitudes and ideologies dominate the groups we belong to[15].

---

[15] Many resources out there aptly describe how our minds work, and how we often become trapped by our cognitive biases and logical fallacies. See Resources for a link that lists them all out beautifully.

Illusions of our own making

+ Group ideologies

--→ = False role-playing in relationships.

From our adherence to a paycheck system for work compensation, to our fascination with fiction and celebrities, to our posturing on social media (and the insistence from the masses to use it!), to our ridiculous worshipping of "time" --- what dominates our social scenes hardly is based on reality.

 Many individuals, teams and organizations, and "communities" operate with The Houdini Complex as its central organizing feature.

SHOW ME A TRICK! *for truth telling*

Central Features of The Houdini Complex, At the Community Level

1. Many people don't know who they really are, what they really want, and what is really in their own best interest.

They outsource their answers to experts, to loved ones, to the unconscious rules and norms of their most valued social group, to a YouTube guru.

2. Many people don't feel safe sharing the truth about their goals, their issues, their feelings, or their real needs in community.

Individuals may share their truth occasionally with a select few people who have earned their trust—but only after proving the conditions are "safe," and truth-telling won't cost them rejection. Once individuals enter social groups and community, most people hide certain parts of themselves.

3. Most people's upbringing and socialization trains them to hide and lie.

Most people don't know how to tell the truth simply because they were never taught how to. When they occasionally did truth tell-tell, they were isolated, rejected, teased, or shaped to conform to another's standards, expectation or ideals.

4. Everyone lies when the desire for being sociable, and appearing to be "good," weighs more heavily than being honest.

Relying on self-reports, especially when it comes to measures of well-being and performance, is woefully flawed. Just considered someone asked you how frequently you smoke, you drink, you speed, you fail a deadline, you lie about something to get out of a commitment. People fudge their self-volunteered data to the detriment of society being well informed on how to improve our wellbeing and social health (32).

5. Most people KNOW that they change, circumstances change, others change, and even die...and yet they spend a lot of effort retaining the illusion that change isn't happening.

Many people understand that things, situations or relationships "don't last forever" and yet when things end or break, they assume something "has gone wrong." So they lie to others and themselves when things are ending, breaking, or aren't seeming sustainable. See Chapter 9 to get familiar with how we are loss averse as a society.

6. Most people secretly admire magicians, tricksters, actors, social media life-stylers.

We all can consciously agree that they people are lying to us. There is a part of us that accepts, tolerates or even enjoys the idea that they "get away with" fooling us publicly.

7. Most people long for at least one safe person that they can tell the complete, unconsciously edited, no-filter truth (64).

Many people don't have any person like this in their lives, unless the arrangement is brief, professional, or one-sided.

8. Many individuals in groups are playing a role that they don't really enjoy, aren't really good at, or can't be sustained without leading to individual or community illness.

Many individuals feel like their role in families and at work isolates us and is a far cry from intimacy with ourselves and others.

Our communities are at a crossroad. We are shifting into different operating systems that are not founded on social comparison, fakery, illusions and deception. conformity, or hierarchical valuation.

The poem, the Houdini Complex strives to highlight that MANY people are aware of duplicity and illusions that dominate our social communities. It spotlights a relationship between someone who is constantly "playing" a certain role, and another who is constantly seeing the real person behind the "play."

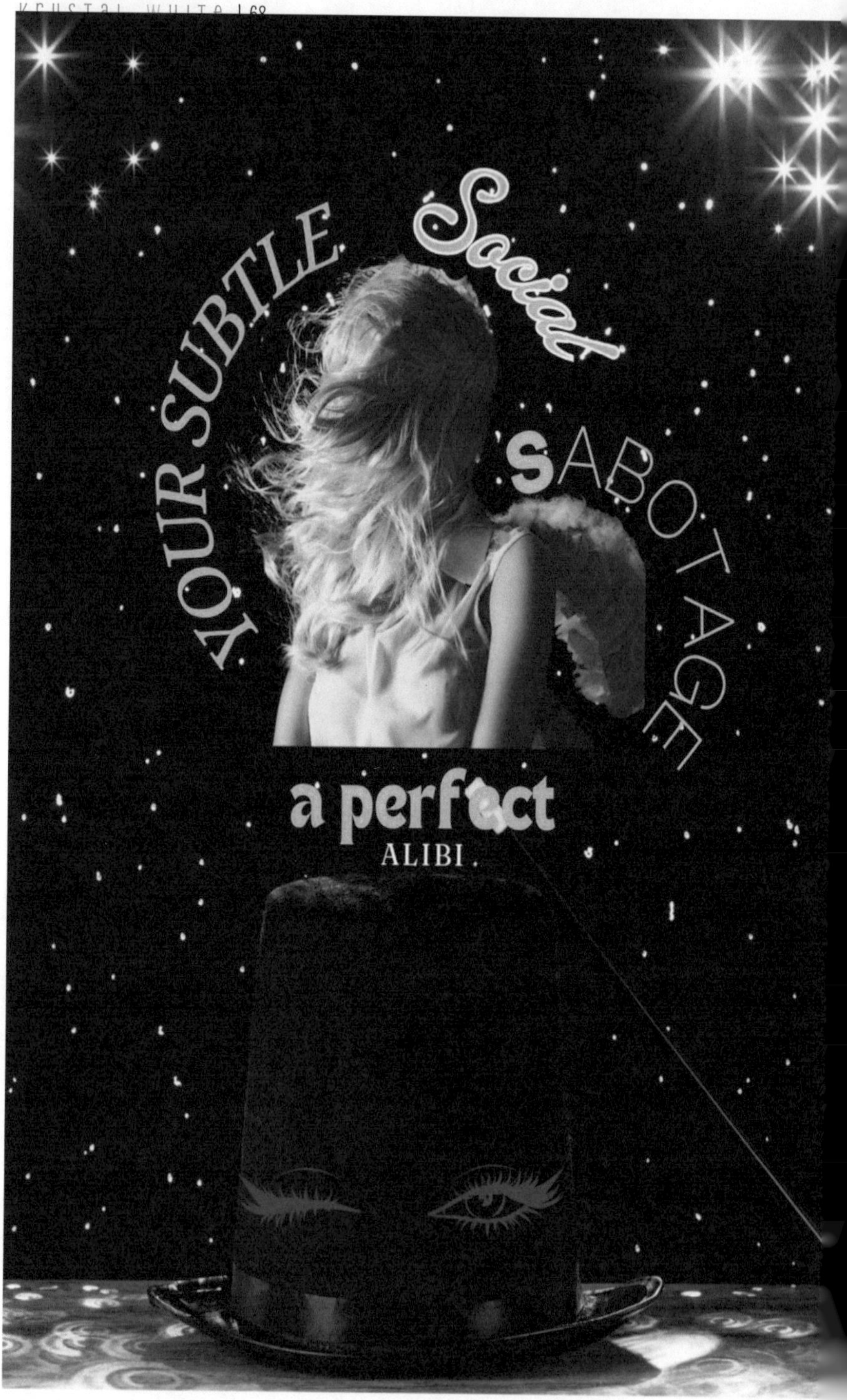
YOUR SUBTLE Social SABOTAGE
a perfect
ALIBI

MANTRAS FOR TRUTH TELLING

I AM NOT BEHOLDEN TO MY STORIES.

I AM NOT BOUND BY THE GOOD INTENTIONS OF OTHERS.

I DO THE SLOW WORK TO SEPARATE THE FACTS OF REALITY FROM MY FEELINGS ABOUT WHAT HAPPENED/IS HAPPENING.

I POINT OUT TO OTHERS CLOSE TO ME WHEN THEY CONFUSE STORIES FOR THEIR TRUTH.

I COMMIT TO THOSE WHO WANT, AND KEEP ME, HONEST.

What are some ways that we in Unconventional Communities can make this shift away from social illusions?

As An Unconventional Citizen

1. Get real about your reality

All mindfulness programs and cognitive behavior therapies start with this basic premise: There is a difference between noticing and thinking. What happened is a fact. We notice facts. What your mind does with what happened is a thought. We make meaning and stories up about reality, and spread them to others, sometimes reactively, and sometimes consciously.

Many people have learned to use a technique called "reframing." Changing your perspective on the facts often improves your feelings and behaviors. Reframing is, and will continue to be, a worthy power tool of mind management. Be mindful of (ha!) its possible potential damage when it is used as a coping mechanism. This occurs when you reframe too frequently an too long in order to tolerate a situation, versus as a tool to change ourselves, or change the situation.[16]

2. Devote yourself to the art of naming and sharing your truth more readily *and* more skillfully.

Decree to:

1) yourself

2) at least one other individual and

3) at least one group in which you belong

that you are intending to tolerate less social masks, "performing," or showing off in order to achieve belonging or affection. Announce that keeping up with illusionary appearances is something you are shifting away from.

Look at your Name your People responses. Select two people from this exercise and one group that you're willing to lead a conversation in truth-telling with.

3. Commit to diversifying social interaction, intimate relating and social contribution---especially in situations and with others where you feel out of your depth, competency level, and groove.

---

[16] Check out the last page of the Handouts Section for a routine exercise on this.

In other words, seek social scenes that shine a light on your imperfections. We all need people and places to help us be conscious of our incompetence in certain skills (whether they are social, emotional, technical or adulting oriented). Imposture syndrome is not something any of us need to be alarmed about, combatting or resisting. It often can be a useful signal for when we're in the perfect situation to mature, gain skills and contribute differently socially.

4. Naming your truth does not mean you share your opinions freely.

Your opinions and perspectives are **not your truth.** Usually they are just thoughts that come and go. Your truth is something more deeply embedded and requires a some deep reflection to unearth. Which means, you don't need to blast out every truth, to everyone, all (most) the time. How much, and when, and with whom we reveal our innermost thoughts, feelings, and actions with relies on your intentions and your social connections. See page 35 if you have not already completed that exercise.

5. Become certified in Mental Health First Aid or Emotional CPR.

The communities of the future will be comprised of citizens who are adept at quickly caring for others who struggle with illusionary relating. Becoming certified as a first-aider is the first step for you to put yourself in a position at a group and community level to ease the suffering related to The Houdini Complex.

These certifiable curriculums are founded on the premise that individual and group mental health often improves through informed and skilled social support. This support relies on non judgmental listening.

If you belong to book meet up, or a learning group of any kind, suggest that the group dives deep into listening skills.

6. Watch your tendency for social isolation.

Needing "a lot of space" from specific others or a specific situation often is a sign you've been faking something, or

IMagine a COMMUNITY WHere YOU were YOUR real, TRUTHFUL SeLF WITH **TWICe aS MaNY PeOPLe** YOU are NOW. IMagine a COMMUNITY WHere YOU were YOUR real, TRUTHFUL SeLF **IN THREE TIMeS aS MaNY grOUPS** aS YOU BeLONg TO NOW. IMagine a COMMUNITY WHere INDIVIDUALS aND grOUPS **FreQUeNTLY NAMED YOU** aS a CITIZeN WHO UPHeLD THIS STANDarD.

THaTS aN UNCONVeNTIONaL COMMUNITY.

avoiding confronting a truth of some kind. Craving alone time often becomes alluring when recovering from The Houdini Complex. Yes—occasional social insulation can be a helpful short-term strategy when re-configuring your "truth." It is not, however, a helpful habit to nurture as a way to escape untenable situations.

Take for example those of you out there who need more spaciousness while interacting. Social situations that are too stimulating, overly expressive, energetically demanding and emotionally exhausting often contribute to introverts needing "space."   The more citizens who express that certain relationships and environments are "too loud," the more our social groups will be able to incorporate shared, quiet chunks of time into their social dynamics.

7.   Protect your Magic.

The magic of the mindful and open heart like you, dear reader, must be protected. It is not meant for the whole world or mass production. If you are the kind of person who wants to share it all with everyone, who must get it all out and lay everything on the table, often the social impact is closing others down: Can they trust you to not publicize what's intimate about them? Do they believe you are discerning? Have you made enough space for them to express themselves too? Is there a structure to channel your sharing to have a point? Is your authenticity dispersed in so many directions that you've lost the magic of the specific, ordinary, 1 of one of a kind moment?

Many of us kill our magic and lead our spirits into demise through the false assumption that we need to be doing "something more" at a bigger, grander scale. The costs of wooing a crowd include "putting on a show" for others. The costs of winning over a lot of people often requires us to focus on being "respectable" over being "truthful."

You know what I'm talking about...right? How you sometimes choose to show up as the respectable one, the good one, the high-road one, the mindful, considerate one versus the one who tells the truth.

Protecting your real magic means guarding it from people who rely on formulas, who need rules to approve of themselves, and who secretly are skeptical of their own magic. Protecting your magic means not succumbing to social comparisons, those you place on yourself or those hoisted on you by others.

Protecting your magic does *not mean* hoarding it for your own consumption. Go back to #6 in the case that you're over isolating your magic in an attempt to protect it.

8. Combine the practice of truth-naming with the discipline of diversifying power.

We can't diversify if people won't claim who they really are, what they really want, and what costs they are willing to pay to keep things the same, or to change. Often, we conform and fail to diversify because we don't want them to know how we act, feel, or think differently. See Chapter 6.

If you don't activate your courageous choice to be more real, and honest, in a social situation—research shows that the other person or people in the group are likely to follow suit. Lying is contagious (61).

Learning how to diversify instead of controlling, conforming or rebelling is the subject of Chapter 6, turn to that page to dive deep into that discipline.

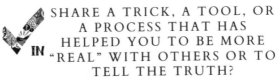

SHARE A TRICK, A TOOL, OR A PROCESS THAT HAS HELPED YOU TO BE MORE "REAL" WITH OTHERS OR TO TELL THE TRUTH?

LISTEN TO SARA SABOURIN. M.A.ED.
EFT PRACTITIONER & CERTIFIED ENERGY HEALER
ANSWER THIS CHECK IN
WWW.LINKEDIN.COM/IN/SARASABOURIN.

As Unconventional Communities

1. Invest in people and programs that efficiently, expertly and with a high level of integrity, teach us to how to "name the truth."

Programs need to do more than educate (giving information and knowledge) on how to tell the truth. They need to actively help us hone the skill and practice it. Blurting out a thought is not the same thing as naming the truth. The latter requires mindfulness *and building a broader capacity* to discern when one is using their higher mind versus lower mind perceptions, beliefs and illusions. Make this education and training accessible, and widely endorsed by social influencers, certification programs, business chambers and local governance. Providing tax incentives or operational or material costs that are funded by grants and corporate donations would likely help spread this capacity more quickly.

2. Instead of emphasizing "truth-telling" in motivational speeches and educational remarks ---thought leaders, managers, and executive staff MUSH prioritize it as an BEHAVIOR and give it public attention.

WHAT DOES TELLING THE TRUTH LOOK LIKE
IN THE GROUPS THAT YOU BELONG TO?

HOW DOES THE GROUP RESPOND WHEN
SOMEONE NAMES WHAT THEY NOTICE? OR
SAYS SOMETHING UNCONVENTIONAL?

WHAT HAPPENS WHEN SOMEONE IS MORE
HONEST THAN RESPECTABLE?

Are points given? Do people publicly credit the person? Do people say "do that more, please" or "I want to do that more, too?" If you're the type of person who says this for others, Free Leadership Inc calls you a leader. Groups that have agreements to reinforce and applaud people who name the truth can mentor others who do not.

It's one thing to say to one another that expressing "truth" and "what's real" is important, and another one that VALUES it **above** political correctness, "respectability," being nice, and magical thinking. Groups and communities that explicitly honor truth-telling either need to learn how to handle, or double down on handling, the typical push back that comes when people encounter the truth.

3. Decrease shared social activities that center around performance, status, social comparison and celebrity culture.

A lot of headway has been made by Brene Brown's work on vulnerability. We are seeing more and more people willing to divulge their "mess" to others. Let's make sure as communities that we are not using "vulnerable sharing" as a way to earn social endorsement. Vulnerability can, and in some situations has, become something we fake, too.

Research shows that faking ability is best understood as a general ability that "people-oriented" people often have in spades. The goal of "faking" anything is to meet a real or perceived, situational demand. People-oriented individuals pick up on these social demands more readily than others. Meaning---if you're the type of person who "naturally reads the room," or the person who you are interacting with, typically you are *more* motivated to, *more* capable of, and take the opportunity to fake it **more** with others than those who don't (33). Those who "read the room" often compare themselves against those who don't more as well. This can trigger them to swing from anger at the social insensitivity of others, to shame in their own lack of confident assertion to "not care what others think so much."

Communities and groups can proactively reduce the motivation of these people in particular to fake their social approval. They can reduce reframing social situations as being "okay" when the situation really needs to be changed. And they can reduce all people-oriented individuals tendencies to distort or avoid their own anger.

4. Cultivate and disseminate non-professional processes and places that value, practice, and constantly process improve both the expression of, and the receiving of, confiding.

We need more people AND groups outside of the therapeutic and recovery industries that offer this discipline and practice. Some research has shown that "invisible support" (e.g. non-professional and social support) often prevents the receiver from experiencing more cognitive distress (32). Many professionals hone the skill of putting in the effort to try to understand what another person is going through, and then helping, when appropriate, in ways that don't minimize or magnify a difficult situation. These skills can be taught and proliferated through our communities with a modicum amount of financial investment.

5. The legal system, and associated groups and individuals who support, use or collaborate with the legal system, can move away from "catching people lying" about bad things they did. Communities can adopt systemic public campaigns to shift the public narrative to reduce lying, "fault" hiding, and fact distortion. Public relations, social media, marketing

and journalism can broader their advocacy of "naming the truth" by discerning truth from opinion in their use of the word. Then they can incentivize stories that don't simply reframe our perspective, they motivate us to actively CHANGE our environment.

Conclusion

Today, my definition of success is becoming better at being me—the realest, most truthful me.

I want to say it's making the lives of others better because I am interacting with them. That definition sounds more socially respectable.

But really—that's not worth it if it comes at the cost of self-betrayal. Plus, it's pretty damaging to us as a collective.

I've had a lot of people disappoint me, let me down, and cause a lot of extra effort or toil or trouble for me when they were following their truth.

They are the ones I look up to today and encourage me to be more and more successful.

Some of them are still the biggest heart-breakers of my life—both professionally and personally. Others of them are the biggest heart-healers of my life—both professionally and personally.

Success is holding them both in equal esteem—while I hold myself to the highest standards of self-sovereignty and prosocial intention.

Imagine a community where you were your real, truthful self with twice as many people you are now.

Imagine a community where you were real, and truthful in THREE times as many groups as you belong to now.

Imagine a community where individuals and groups frequently NAMED you as a citizen who upheld this standard.

Imagine a community that taught you how to do that.

That's an Unconventional Community.

If both citizens and communities committed to these goals, together we would be more capable, more ready and more willing to practice truth-telling over imposture praising.

The Bright Ideas of Others

How can communities help us share our truths versus hide behind social masks? I'd love for communities to loudly and proudly represent themselves as especially open and welcoming to new people.

A dedicated community rep may greet newcomers, spend a

few minutes one to one, asking questions and taking the time to listen, understand who is showing up and their reasons for it - needs or wants - and share this with the community, offering a frictionless introduction to the community, and the community to the individual.

Keith Elliss

https://www.linkedin.com/in/keithellis84

HOW CAN COMMUNITIES HELP US SHARE OUR TRUTHS VERSUS HIDE BEHIND SOCIAL MASKS?

The things I feel I need to hide behind a mask, when I enter into community, I see that other people also have those things — and this helps me feel the things I have to hide are actually normal!

CULTIVATE groups where people can share openly & VULNERABLY. This helps others who may NOT FEEL COMFORTABLE Being VULNERABLE to CONNECT with others who they can relate to on a DEEPER LEVEL.

When communities hold a safe space for people to show up as their authentic selves, there's an opening for love, connection, and a newness. It takes humans to a deeper level when that happens.

How do hide your feelings, concerns, perspectives, needs & ideas from others?

WHAT TYPES OF PEOPLE DO YOU BECOME LESS
PRESENT, LESS REAL OR LESS TRUTHFUL AROUND?

_____

_____

_____

_____

WHAT DO YOU BELIEVE YOU GAIN FROM HIDING?

_____

_____

_____

_____

_____

WHAT HELPS YOU TELL THE TRUTH?

_____

_____

_____

_____

_____

notes

CHAPTER 4

SIT ON THE SIDELINES SOMEWHERE ELSE

Towards More Social Ownership

Most people can read, they can study, they can write, they can listen, they can practice, and they can assert their agency.

Despite a very strong emotional incentive to express one's agency, and a deep value for wanting to make decisions that make us feel good, communities face a handful of conundrums:

1) Many people's drive for agency often results in negative outcomes. What they predict will make them feel good often doesn't, especially long term (6)

2) Stress, un-health, and imperceptible social pressure distorts our thoughts and our actions around agency. (7)

3) Agency does not lead to, nor is equated, with social ownership (8).

Let's just assume you believe in the concept of free will (which in and of itself, is a philosophical assumption that has not been proven by science) (9). Free will, broken down into its most simple translation means that:

You have *the capacity to choose* and you've got choices.

Behavioral psychologists call this capacity: agency.

Now, that "capacity to choose," our agency, isn't static, and can be manipulated, influenced, and environmentally wired. Whatever is not you—living things (people and nature), tangible things (objects, possessions) and non-tangible things (like ideas, dreams, visions, beliefs, feelings, energies) can foster or limit your agency. You (your thoughts, feelings, experiences and actions) can also foster or limit your agency.

Your agency waxes and wanes based on certain biological, neurological and hormonal patterns and one-off occurrences within your physical functioning.

All these facts add up to quite an intriguing pill to swallow given that your choices have consequences.

All the different ideologies and attitudes folks adopt and proliferate have different suggestions, opinions and preferences for how people **should** be using their agency. Some people devote their lives to promoting the agency of others. Some people devote their lives to controlling the agency of others. Some people devote their lives attending mostly to their own agency. Some people devote their lives oblivious to their agency at all.

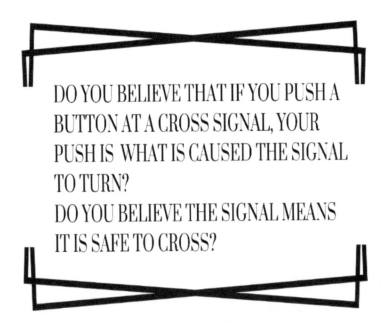

DO YOU BELIEVE THAT IF YOU PUSH A BUTTON AT A CROSS SIGNAL, YOUR PUSH IS WHAT IS CAUSED THE SIGNAL TO TURN?
DO YOU BELIEVE THE SIGNAL MEANS IT IS SAFE TO CROSS?

The **exact same sentiment applies to** a *lack of agency.*

Simply just read that entire paragraph again (e.g. Some people devote their lives controlling the **lack of** agency of others) and the importance of "agency" in social contexts will start to become crystal clear to you.

Hmmmmm.

All this discussion, focus and emphasis around agency and its impact is not going away. Agency is at the heart of mindfulness movement, which lays the foundation to establish and master emotional intelligence. Emotional intelligence is the precursor to influence. Unless you are mindful of your agency and impact and are committed to understanding and managing yourself and others (EI), you cannot willfully channel yourself as an instrument of influence.

The fastest way to influence each other is to understand, and predict, what I/You/We need—and then act with agency to meet those needs.

WILL YOU BECOME
AN AGENT
for Unconventional Communities?

This book you're taking in right now can be, and possibly is, one way for you, or groups, to become more capable of influencing, or shifting, group norms. It requires your activated sense of agency in order to read it.

Here's the thing—it is not enough to believe in, curate, or hone **_solely_** our agency. When the conversation overly emphasizes "agency" and "choices," we quickly become exhausted (both individually and in our groups). We often feel that we have little to show for our efforts, and always left with more and more work to do.

We can always continue to value, re-assess, and reclaim our agency. But now it's time for us to level up and move beyond its dominating focus. Individuals and groups would benefit from reducing their clutch hold, and dogmatism around it.

Otherwise, we will have very little band-with to examine our individual, group and community relationship ***with ownership***.

WHAT DO YOU REALLY OWN?
NAME ALL THE THINGS THAT TRULY BELONG TO YOU.

Who or what owns you?? Do you belong to?

Ownership in and of itself requires that 1) you <u>hold something</u> (a possession, a feeling, an idea, a possession, a project or plan, a goal, a person) in a way that 2) it belongs to you.

I know, or I can feel some of you reading this starting to cringe.

Many of us belong to groups that have a ***very dark past*** relationship with ownership. The immaturity, brutality and unquestionable violence associated with "ownership" still runs in most of our blood lines, collective psychologies, and personal shadows.

Now is the time we as a community resolve these past issues and move towards a renovated relationship with ownership. While, there may be *many, many, many* factors (especially those that are unconscious to us) that limit our AGENCY, there are only a few, however, that can limit our OWNERSHIP.

Ownership **REQUIRES a conscious choice.** We may have " borrowed" a few things without our awareness…and those borrowed things of course have power. But we don't *really* **"own"** them, right? Whether those things are lessons/materials, podcasts, books, ideals, lifestyles, values, goals, wounds, weapons, hopes, dreams, methodologies, roles, agreements---the only way for you to truly own something is by agreeing to, and sustaining your responsibility, to OWN it.

Our world doesn't continue to endure suffering, injustice, polarization and war because we have not tried, or because we don't use, agency. It doesn't cry out because we have not chosen to fix things. **Our world hurts, our society hurts, because we (both individuals and groups) do not own it.**

We hurt because we have not been taught how to socially own things, with honor.

Not only that, our world and society suffer now because we have not been taught how to proactively own something without subsuming its essence or invading its natural boundaries.

We have not been shown how to commit to something's best interest *without it costing us ours*. We have not been shown how to trust others to be responsible for us without **MASSIVE** disappointment, and we have not been shown to have people, places, and things "belong to us" while also honoring its agency.

If you're considering your own personal life right now…you're exactly where you belong. If you're feeling the pain of "mother nature" and humanity, that makes complete sense.

This common-place lack of ownership runs, and cuts, deep. It mostly chokes the trust that could potentially be built. And trust is the conscious breath of connection.

Research from multiple fields indicates that trust is required for relationships that serve the well-being of all involved. Those who hold trust possess the most valuable and sustainable resource of modern society.

Ownership itself is a conscious choice to be responsible for the impact you have. While communities may have no shortage of individuals who are named leaders, or call themselves leaders, we may have only a handful of high-quality ones that commit to the discipline of honorable ownership.

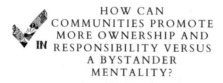

HOW CAN COMMUNITIES PROMOTE MORE OWNERSHIP AND RESPONSIBILITY VERSUS A BYSTANDER MENTALITY?

LISTEN TO BUSINESS. COUPLES AND LIFE COACH ERIC NUTTING ANSWER THIS CHECK IN.

The poem *How the Shaman Broke Up with Me* is more about a failure of ownership than a failure of intimacy.

The poem is a twist on a Dear John letter—what people did in previous cultural eras before technical ghosting was common. The body uses the voice of the shaman, explaining why the relationship is over; the title indicates that the person who was left has decided to publicly share with about it.

There is widespread diversity on how to define high quality leadership. This diversity is very helpful, and necessary, as communities have different social values, different social wounds, different social resources and gaps, and different physical assets and limitations.

The problem is—very few groups and communities define and publish "this is what a leader looks like around here."

WHAT DOES A LEADER LOOK LIKE IN THE
GROUP YOU WORK WITH?
IN YOUR NEIGHBORHOOD?
IN YOUR FAMILY?

The shaman doesn't tell us her/his definition either. Instead, her letter reads like both a prescription and a complaint. The readers can only assume that the shaman believed his/her partner either passively rejected his own ownership and personal power, or that he failed to make visible efforts to proactively be an owner of the relationship.

The shaman is not there anymore, and the letter doesn't mention anything about her own part in the dysfunction. Instead of having a conversation, she chooses to deliver the message as she is leaving.

Sometimes, endings show us what the story of a relationship was all about.[17]

The receiver of the message, however, is the one who openly shares it with others. Is the receiver attempting to lead, to own things now, in this way?

The poem asks all of us to question:

- How have I contributed to creating "our" current reality?
- Who owns what?

---

[17] See Chapter 8 to dive deep into the power of endings.

- How, or where, am I on the sidelines?

I personally squirm when I read this poem out loud. It gets under my skin. It asks for an unflinching look at all the ways I avoid ownership. It wants me to see how I can disempower others to own what belongs to them.

Many individuals may take responsibility and leadership in their one-to-one relationships, and *some* take *some* ownership in *some* of the groups they "belong to."

Few:

1) **know how to or**

2) **have the encouragement to, and/or**

3) **actively choose to,**

take ownership in the communities that they draw resources from and live in.

I frequently use a line a mentor used on me years ago: "where's your DNA on this?" in many of the leadership development programs I facilitate.

Perhaps the shaman realizes how she has been contributing to less power, less engagement and less ownership in her partner by staying together and waiting it out. Confusion, blame and waiting for someone else to change are clever ways to defend against the call towards ownership.

The other ways to avoid ownership involve a handful of moral disengagement mechanisms.

Moral Disengagement Mechanisms Include:

Moral Justification: Using worthy ends or moral purposes to sanctify immoral behavior

Euphemistic Labeling: Labeling the immoral behavior in a way that makes it sound less negative or more respectable

Diffusion of responsibility: Diluting personal responsibility due to the presence of other people

Dehumanization: Stripping the victim of human qualities and equal values, and projecting exaggerated labels onto them

Blaming the victim: Believing that the victim deserves his or her pain, problems and or suffering.

Many individuals cannot see and accept all the ways they are contributing to the well-being of others either, particularly if they 1) aren't paid for these contributions 2) aren't effectively and routinely recognized for these contributions and 3) struggle with owning their talents, gifts and accomplishments.

Consider how common these dynamics are for you in your groups and communities.

How are you contributing to your community's dysfunction?

How are you contributing to its well-being?

Central Features of Sideline Membership, At the Community Level

1. Reinforced bystanding.

Research has shown that more and more people are overwhelmed, ill equipped and disinterested in tackling complicated social issues. Moral disengagement is associated both with passive bystanding, or failing to act when an action could be helpful. In one on one relationships, it is associated with persistent stonewalling, breaking off communication, staying silent, and withdrawing emotionally or physically. At a community level, behaviors such as ghosting, gossiping, turning a blind eye to your own/your group's, unhelpful social behaviors, dominate the scene.

2. Shallow Engagement Norms.

Most people equate engagement with likes, comments, and chatter. The actual word means a pledge of some kind. In our current society, we have watered down engagement to literally describe the minimal amount of input a person can give, with very little personal investment or commitment. As research begins to tweeze out how and when our usage of social media, impacts our mental well-being,

3. Social disengagement trends.

Research shows that our personal engagement, and disengagement, is highly influenced by our peer group. More and more communities, and especially organizational workforce, *report a common belief* that disengagement is common, and rising. This belief in and of itself quickly influences others to disengage.

Personal and group social disengagement has been shown to negatively impact almost all well-being measures: physical vitality, business wealth, relational satisfaction, environmental health, criminal acts, and social justice. Disengagement of mass proportion sets the foundation for social isolation—which has literally been shown to change not only our brain functioning, but our long-term brain development.

4.   Polarized moral values.

This characteristic is either self-explanatory and/or I'm choosing not to spend my attention here on explaining it further. ☹

5.   Childish leader selection.

How we see and select leaders today reflects the cognitive maturity of children. What kind of leader communities select is influences by transitory collective psychologies and individuals using cognitive biases, faulty logic and/or emotional logic. Emotional logic is when we making a decision primarily with our feelings, and then later justifying it with a reason (10).

There is evidence that in times of high conflict, war and dissension, research subjects prefer candidates that appear older, with more masculine facial features and assertive expressions (11). During times of more harmony, well-being and peace, they prefer younger, more feminine facial features, and calm expressions. Even more remarkable—kids (ages 5 to 13) pick the winner of obscure elections 71% of the time…just based on pictures (12). 😲

6. Evading Responsibility.

Most people don't wake up aiming to shirk responsibility. The fact is, most people simply do not have the tools to handle differences, disagreements, upsets and diversion in a way that leads to cohesion, social growth, collective well-being , or justice.

The vast majority of psychologists, organizational experts, community organizers, spiritual and religious figures and thought leaders all agree: conflict must be acknowledged, addressed and resolved in order to prevent deadlock, dis-ease and unnecessary break down.

Some also consider conflict *a necessary ingredient or step towards the well-being of a diversified "US"* (13).

Many people go into well-meaning and even prosocial groups or a community that espouses collaboration only to encounter that there's really only a select few who call the shots.

When you look at what's happening at a community level, many people:

- Become crusaders for a specific cause…doing whatever it takes, whatever is costs, to win the war against "XYZ".

- Most people give up, losing, allowing the winners to dictate reality. (See Chapter X, which explores dichotomous winner/losers relating).

If we don't attempt to win/conquer/prove and we don't give up, we have already committed a lot of blood, sweat and tears into the process of trying to work together.

The cognitive load, the consistent effort and the deliberate management of relationship needs and self ego checking and the slow progress become really overwhelming.

It makes sense that the next course of action MOST people do (especially when it comes to community) is to DELEGATE decisions, and therefore confrontation, to someone else. Citizens and groups feel relieved to pass the buck to a higher authority when their efforts to attempt to collaborate towards resolution don't work.

A lot of the time, that "authority" *does solve* the issue for them—not necessarily efficiently, and not necessarily to every one's best interest. Often, when we turn to community leaders (like government, the institution, the experts, the big man) only a mere fraction of the community wins, and the risk is, all others lose.

Many people and many groups reinforce a cognitive bias that those who "govern" community are in the best position to make community wise decisions. Or to make the point clearer—many people have a bias that those who are

- Elected or selected
- and are deferred to

have the MOST responsibility to make community wide decisions. They hold onto this belief even when there is clear evidence to the contrary (14). So they delegate to them.

What most people and groups haven't grasped is that the solution is: to NOT to delegate key decisions, at least not automatically.

Why is active engagement, and active playing in the game of relationships and community life so rare?

- Most people and many groups don't understand how to, or they don't choose to invest in, a life-style where their well-being is NOT delegated to a higher authority.
- Most people and many groups don't know how to, or they don't choose to invest in, a life-style where everyone plays, and everyone plays to win.

Our communities are at a nexus point.

Communities need new ways to foster ownership, leadership and prosocial community responsibility.

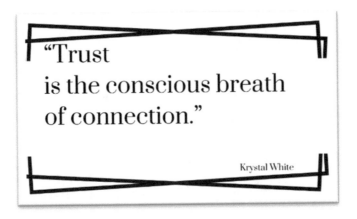

"Trust is the conscious breath of connection."

Krystal White

Many of us realize that we desire a shift as a community away from Sideline Citizenship. Here's how we can do that:

As An Unconventional Citizen

1. Be a willing, capable and ready "owner."

Do this mentally. Understand that being active in your groups, relationship and community requires you to own that you are a valued resource. Invest in cognitive inventories or exercises that help you get clear, confident and an owner of your strengths, relational skills, and techniques you have mastered. They belong to you. Therefore, you must care for them. Every 6 months, re-asses what roles, features and goals still belong to you. Write these out on index cards and place in easy to find locations, create scheduled technological

Own your time.

Every 6 months, examine where you are spending your physical time---how much time are you on the couch, transportation, office, nature, meetings, hobbies, home, new environmental terrain. Where does your body prefer to be?

Are your routines or habits physically needing tweaking in order for you to be a ready and awesome player? Invest in movement and recovery disciplines that honor your body's need for work, play, study and rest.

Every 6 months, examine where you are spending your social time---how much time are you having fun with others, deeply sharing and deeply listening to others, collaborating on a project with others, changing up your roles and agreements with others? List out Who and where are you resting, playing, working and studying with?

Do your physical or social time investment need slight shifts?

reminders on your calendars, and also verbalize them in your trusted groups.

Do this physically. Understand that being active in your groups, relationship and community requires you to act like a valued resource. The #1 one way you can ensure this is by following through with your **chosen** roles and agreements. This requires proactive active agreement setting in the first place*. Agree to play roles that you are ready, able and willing to play NOW. Ask for, and actively seek obtaining, the resources you need to do that role well. Identify what you are NOT ready, capable or willing to do in this role.

2. Refuse to delegate.

Especially 1) in situations where the upset, the issue, or the relationship *really* matters to you personally and 2) to leaders, systems, industries, organizations and initiatives who you haven't earned, kept and are still committed to, your trust in their leadership.

3. Watch out for, and limit, mental short-cuts.

In relationships, groups, and communities we often sideline ourselves, or others, when heuristics, or mental short-cuts, dominate our "play book." These are called cognitive biases and logical fallacies. [18] Examples: 1) we equate being effective, or being knowledgeable, with being a good leader (questionable cause) 2) we assume those in authority positions have better answers than we do (authority bias).

Pointing out when logical fallacies and cognitive biases are present in the groups you belong to and in the groups you interact with, will proliferate more conscientious decision making.

As Unconventional Communities

1. Vote for Leadership Definition.

Instead of getting individuals and groups to endorse specific candidates, communities can get them to vote on the top three or four attributes of a high quality leader. I have lead many organizational campaigns to establish these cultural definitions, and many other organizational development specialists, intentional communities and executive teams are doing this awesome work right now. This model surely is founded on many native tribes and councils of the past, with a proven track record of high-trust, highly sustainable interactions between people and "their leaders." Extending this model to the community level is imperative if we are

---

[18] See Resources for an easy to use handout you can use in your relationships, teams and community circles to educate each other.

going to cultivate leaders that serve the consensus versus their political party. What if every four years the population needed to vote on those components of a high quality leader, ensuring that shifts were made to reflect the current realities and the near future needs? What if all the candidates, regardless of their party affiliation or credentials, went through an initial vetting process to ensure that their character reflected the community's definition of a leader, as defined by the population (versus defined by the candidate). How would that change our perspective of politics, the selection process of decision makers, and reduce polarizing side-line jeering?

2. Introduce Circular leadership.

This occurs when *every* person on the team must hold the position as the key decision maker for a duration long enough for the *entire* group to build trust in that person as a key player and leader. Read that sentence again. Imagine how team-work would be different if this standard was achieved more frequently than it is today.

Diversify Players. Players in unconventional communities come in all shapes, sizes, skills, ages, and costumes. There are no "old" players. There are only those whose concepts are hardened. There are no "first string" players. There are only those who are over-relied on and over-worked. If communities ensured that the underworked are resourced well and relied upon for their contribution, the overworked would be protected from ego driven burn out, victimization, and entitlement (now, or later).

3. Create and Measure Shared Wins.

The best team games measure shared points, shared infractions and shared awards. Instead of measuring everyone's scores by themselves, and aggregating them together, shared wins are reliant on collaborative efforts. Communities that create, or use, both individual AND group indicators of well-being or dysfunction, can factor in both individual and group engagement into their well-being indexes. There are awesome examples of this in the Blue Zone Community Research and Initiatives*

4. Double Down on the Ownership Conversations:

Peter Block's Community describes 5 key conversations for us all to master. The Ownership Conversation is the most fitting for cultivating active leadership. Communities that master this conversation not only foster accountability, they compel interdependence. Groups can do master this conversation, for sure…however, when the **most groups within a** community master and practice it together, that's when our collective well being will be tangibly observed and easily measured. Some example questions that inspire ownership: What has our group done to contribute to the very thing we complain about or want to change? How important to me/our group is this [initiative, relationship, issue, area]? How much risk, how much effort, how much time, are will willing to take? How involved are we capable of and willing to be?

Conclusion

This is it. We can no longer afford a dynamic where most of us are sitting on the sidelines. We can not continue telling other people to be engaged and own their well-being when we aren't willing to be in the game with them ourselves. No more sitting on the sidelines, unless we're resting and recovering so that you can get back in there!

Here's to us playing the game, making up new rules and awards for the game, and playing it well as a team.

The Bright Ideas of Us

How can communities promote more social ownership?

Why not pay or somehow incentivize (tax break, lower utilities) social influencers that model community involvement and active engagement as much as they receive from promoting products on Instagram or Amazon?

--Random quick thought from a fellow coffee shop customer.

WE DISTRIBUTE MANUALS FOR

HOME, CAR, AND BUSINESS OWNERSHIP.

none for self-ownership.

Communities can create local guidebooks for personal and relational well-being

those that participate and tax the ones who are not as engaged without good reasons.

ANDY CONSTANTINE

HOW CAN COMMUNITIES BETTER PROMOTE OWNERSHIP AND SOCIAL RESPONSIBILITY ?

Feeling that your vote matters → more voting → more ownership
Ensuring that it isn't operating like a "totem pole" vs. a circle.
USE the voice of the community to decide what is best for the community.

Chapter 5

NO ONE WILL CONVINCE THEM THAT LOVE AND ATTENTION ARE THE SAME THING.

Towards Love More Over Fear

I'm the type of person who gets overly excited over miniature condiments, new shoots on my house plants and bites of food with strange flavor combinations. I'm in love with my popcorn maker, and frequently express my adoration about it publicly. I extrovert my joy about fast moving lines to strangers in the grocery store.

These habits have nothing to do with love, though. At least not the kind of love we're going to be attending to in this chapter. The kind we're talking about is the social kind--- social love that is achieved through peace, trust, harmony, joy, excitement, awe and/or pleasure. [19]

I've always respected people who set out to LOVE themselves more like they were learning how to play the guitar. I've

---

[19] See the image on page 109 to learn about the different pathways towards love.

always been jealous of those who chose LOVE as their word for the year, not having to even think about it. I've always been mystified by those who identify LOVE as their primary value and appear to let it rule the day.

I've occasionally been mistaken for a competent self-lover. I try to remind people that I love my life, and I love the living—for the life of me, however, I've never quite mastered the hang of loving myself.

It's not that I'm a tough cookie. My penchant for flowery, flowing words and my unwavering value for "the truth as we know it," leaves my heart crumbly, mushy, tenderized most days. I'm not a captain of a "self-love ship" yet because there have been so many other vehicles to commander, and "love" for myself was not a foreign language available in school.

Someone once told me that my capacity to love myself was equal to my capacity to love others.

Her school must have offered a class, explaining that specific math more in depth. I'm positive she received helpful lessons about how to self-love I didn't.

Here's the thing: As much as I want to center love, to focus on love, to attend to love, for love to be the thing that wins, that saves us, that reminds us to be good to one another, that ushers in a fresh solar system and rules over gravity:

I live with the fact that I was taught to survive, to out-fight, to out-wit, to out-perform, to out-run, to out-hide and to out-fear. Adults who left me home alone literally said: "Don't burn the house down." They didn't say: "Tell yourself loving things tonight".

"HOW TO BE(COME) GOOD" was the lesson taught at home, in school, at work, and in relationships. How to love, how to be loved, how to let love take center stage, those all were off to the side, the earned treat for (finally!) being good, or sanctioned for major holiday messages and the real lives of more holy people.

Listen, there's no blame here or judgement here. Pointing fingers regarding the messages and the values of such an environment is not an effective healing strategy. The true point here is that despite some social trends to love ourselves, honor ourselves and rewire our minds towards love, it doesn't take center stage during our day to day interactions.

How much money did you spend on love this week?

What percentage of your overall waking hours where spent on love?

If you were genuinely asked by a person you trusted: "Do you love your life?" how would you respond?

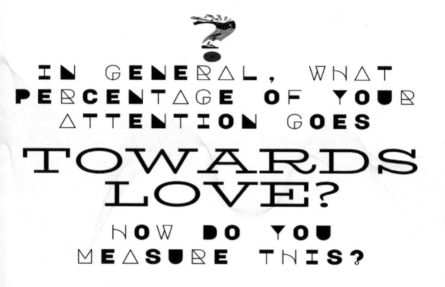

IN GENERAL, WHAT PERCENTAGE OF YOUR ATTENTION GOES

TOWARDS LOVE?

HOW DO YOU MEASURE THIS?

Can I Have Your Attention Please?[20]

As this book is being written in Spring of 2024, it is evident that individuals, groups and communities believe that they can quickly and easily distinguish their attention to things they love and they don't love. What *they actually are paying*

---

[20] I stole this line from a section header in Check In. See that chapter for a brief summary on how social attention works.

attention to are things that "feel good" and things that annoy them, drain them, challenge them, sadden them and especially those that—trigger fear in them. Fear is sticky in terms of getting our attention. It is quite easy to see and it's quite easy to spread.

> Love is not the opposite of fear, by the way. They aren't anchors of, or occupy the extreme ends of any reputable energy spectrum. Spiritual experts, energy masters and the most educated and devoted academic scientist can't actually agree on "what love is" --that's how little we have studied it or that our "studies" have produced.

Communities are on the tippy-top-point of the iceberg of advanced, accessible and quickly computed information that can also be easily dispersed. Right now, many populations are generating AI related products and proliferating them throughout our remote and physical environments.

We're witnessing a new way of doing life in our community that will have *significant, unexpected and revolutionary impact on how and what we attend to.*

We have the opportunity to tip the scales towards attending to MORE of what we value, desire and long to contribute to OVER what problems are present, what we fear, and what we want to avoid. This period of time is akin to how the McDonalds franchise revolutionized eating out for the global community; the ease and ROI of fast/cheap food dissemination married to tasty morsels that most humans couldn't help but LOVE (at least initially).

Starbucks followed a similar model, pairing its competence at creating a "third space" with warm, caffeinated and sugary beverages that appealed to mass audiences. Foam and steamed milk were introduced and then normalized, globally, with impressive speed. From the years 1998-2008, over 1 trillion cups in over 500 countries were consumed; and over 4000 stores were established (15). Gather a group of 8 people and you'll find one who is excited when Pumpkin Spice season comes around, or has spent more than 100 hours socializing, writing or world-wide-webbing at a coffee shop, or has attempted to replicate the same energy at home in some way.

If we can spread burgers and latte that people love and consume, we surely can do the same with love.

Perhaps you as an individual, or a group that you are affiliated with, is discussing and experimenting with 1) programming 2) understanding 3) "mastering" and/or 4) collaborating using/with AI.

There is a vast difference between populations that USE AI and those that work WITH AI. Just as there is a vast difference between those who use humans and those who work with humans.

Humans working with AI, and with one another, can absolutely seize this opportunity to alter our social norms away from its foundation on fear and a shallow, superficial, hedonistic adoption of "love." We can and some of us are called to facilitate communities that center their attention on pragmatic, comprehensive and diverse expressions of "Love."

What if our communities in the future believed and practiced that love and attention are the same thing?

What if **that** was a primary community goal---to center love as a focal point? What if our "systems" were set up to facilitate love and attention being so aligned, that distinguishing them would be difficult?

I believe that achievement requires revolutionary education about love and a maturity of relational skills.

Ever since that line was published in Unconventional Citizens in 2022, numerous people have queried about this line: NO ONE WILL CONVINCE THEM THAT LOVE

AND ATTENTION ARE THE SAME THING. Some pushed back about it, and some ignored it completely.

are Love and attention the same thing to you?

They aren't, not for most people, today.

We cannot be convinced; there is too much data to the contrary. Most people believe that the things that get their attention frequently are NOT the things they really love.

Many people have the belief that their attention is held hostage by their surroundings, which often don't contain a lot of love. They report requiring a lot of effort, training and support in order to focus their attention and intentions on what really matters to them.

The poem, *Stop Looking at Me,* is about this common conundrum—how our attention has been trained less on what we love, and more trained on what we fear.

It re-frames the classic myth of Medusa and Perseus. It doesn't tell you directly what it's about for a reason—love often gets obscured by our personal stories, our collective norms and fairy tales, and historical mis-uses of power.

LISTEN TO

ALL EYES ON ME

The graphic preceding the poem offers a clue into "the unseen" storyline and the poem's key point: Until now, the truth of love is often NOT what gets published and proliferated throughout the community. .The myths about love, as well as those about heart-break, dominate our community energy and often drive our attention. There are many features about "how we love" that remain hidden and unseen to us.

In society today, most individuals struggle to be truly seen by others. Most people struggle to truly see others. Many find that "seeing" (in-to-me-see) whether into our own selves or another human, especially triggering.

As we already covered in Chapters 3 and 4, our social media platforms, real-world interactions and entertainment options often set us up to be superficial bystanders and adept comparison bingo players. Our communities set us up to have intimacy incompetencies and offer very few resources that can help us quickly overcome our intimacy challenges.

I won't retell the classical myth of Medusa here. I predict a screenplay or book to be published in the near future that retells the story in modern terms. Perhaps it will be another story of Divine Feminine power being revealed and revered; one where a persecuted underdog better understands, and then channels, her talents and capacities towards humanity's well-being.

We will see. Ha!

What I *will tell* you here is that the inspiration for the poem came from a series of connected experiences. In August 2021, I did a few meditations that concretely involved Medusa; I started dreaming about her. Strangely, within that same week, my friend showed me his artistic rendering of Luciano Garbati's statue.

The next week, I got up at 0330 in the morning to witness the constellation of Perseus showering down meteorites. These synchronized experiences together compelled me to write the poem out the same day. I created my own fiction about Medusa and Perseus: One where the relationship was not predicated on war, on killing a powerful thing in order to win the favor of a powerful God, or on humanity's

attention being founded on what we fear. Instead of killing

Medusa, or Medusa beheading Persuses (like the statue), in my poem Perseus had fallen in love with Medusa. He couldn't help but look at her, and to love her.

It was love, not the frightening spell of snake hair, that "froze" him alive.

The poem is about the kind of love that freezes your attention.

And for a moment of time, love and attention are the same thing.

Many people in our communities steadfastly and without contemplation, follow "feeble fables," especially those about love. The field of romance fiction is a billion dollar industry that trumps all other genres. When it comes to films, Adventure, Action and Drama films generate the most revenue, however more than 70 percent of time, those films have a "love story line" embedded in them.

We are trained to "See" love as "love" when it fits into a certain narrative, and most other social narratives center themselves around fear (especially fear of being the "broken girl" or the "bad guy.")

In my poem, Medusa understands that both those who fear her AND those who love her, will fictionalize her. She reciprocates love to Perseus anyway. She acknowledges it, holds it, and squirms from it. She implores those who look at her, especially Perseus, to stop.

Love is something dangerous—it breaks things before it makes things.

When love and attention are the same thing, the fiction we hold about ourself will be broken.

When love and attention are the same thing, the fiction we hold about the other will be broken.

When love and attention are the same thing, the fiction we create about love will be something we want to hold onto.

How communities can channel their shared attention to love is what this chapter is about.

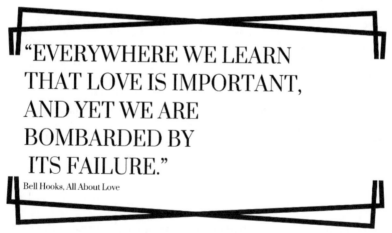

"EVERYWHERE WE LEARN THAT LOVE IS IMPORTANT, AND YET WE ARE BOMBARDED BY ITS FAILURE."

Bell Hooks, All About Love

Are you attending to a life that you love?

If love is so important, we must admit to ourselves how incompetent we are as a community, in many of our groups, and as individuals at ATTENDING to it.

Central Features of Unattended Love, At the Community Level

1. Polarizing, Confusing Messages.

Communities typically espouse extremely polarized versions of love...either it heals everything, and triumphs over all, or is hurts us, disappoints us, lures us in the wrong direction.

2. Relegated to pair bonding. Another person cannot possibly meet all our needs for belonging and love.

Generating love is usually the responsibility of religion, spirituality or the arts rather than science, commerce, education, and technology. Other industries do not attend to it as a central theme.

3. Love is an aspirational feeling versus a skill.

Most people label love as an emotion. In fact, in a research study asking people to rate words on a scale of 1-5 (1 I definitely would not call this an emotion, 5 I definitely would call this an emotion), love receives the highest marks---3.94....slightly over the definitiveness of hate 3.90. Most people and groups want to feel love rather than practice it.

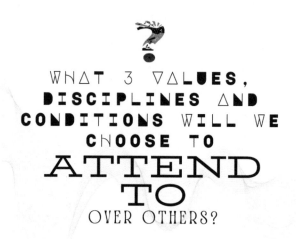

WHAT 3 VALUES,
DISCIPLINES AND
CONDITIONS WILL WE
CHOOSE TO
ATTEND
TO
OVER OTHERS?

WHAT FEELINGS WILL
THESE GENERATE?

Our communities are ready to shift in the direction of joy, trust, peace, pleasure, excitement, gratitude and awe.

Many of us realize that we desire a shift as a community away from unattended love. Communities need new narratives about love, and new ways that make attending to it, skillfully generating it and using technology to spread it, the norm.

How can we do that:

As An Unconventional Citizen

1. Bust your Love Myths.

Do you know what love means to you **today**? Name all the things you believed about love as a teenager, love in your 20s, love pre-COVID 19, love last year…that you don't believe today. Do you know what fables you follow? There are many resources to help you personally define and clarify with compassion what love means and looks like to you **right now**, as well as what conditions you can ask for or create in order to experience more of it. Attending to love requires that you proactively name and create those conditions for yourself. When reality diverges from those conditions, that you take them as opportunities to keep learning, re-writing and re-wiring love for yourself. Sharing your new and updated beliefs with others is one awesome way to collectively attend to more love. Your love myths are meant to be shared with those you choose to let in. See our resources section. (16 The Letter Code).

2. Attend to how you love.

As a very basic level, we arrive at the "feeling of love" through repetitive and **recognized** feelings (**aka "we see them"**). neuropsychological processes that are reinforced and one's environment in early life, set us up to prefer ONE pathway over the other in order to "get to" love. The preferences can shift during certain periods of life and due to other environmental contexts.

Functional imaging research on the brains of monks and other highly skilled spiritual practitioners report high levels of "love" in all these areas while their brain is lit up. Knowing our usual way of doing something can help us attend to other ways of doing something. The more options and choices we have for experiencing love at an individual level, the greater likelihood that we will reinforce it at a group and community level. Not to mention that we will be less judgmental when those around us get to love in a different way.

LOVE MORE, OVER FEAR

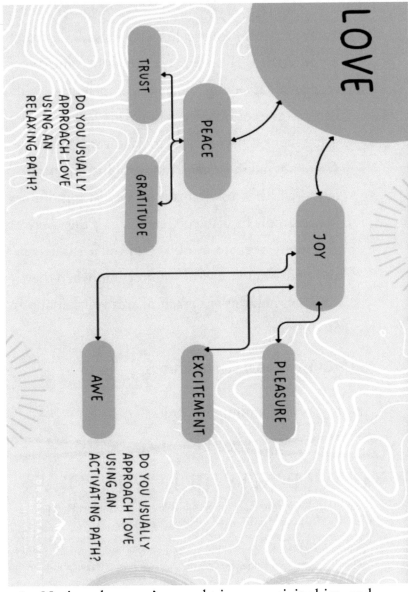

LOVE

TRUST

PEACE

GRATITUDE

JOY

AWE

EXCITEMENT

PLEASURE

DO YOU USUALLY
APPROACH LOVE
USING AN
RELAXING PATH?

DO YOU USUALLY
APPROACH LOVE
USING AN
ACTIVATING PATH?

3. Notice when you're caught in a negativity bias, and
   unconsciously attending to fear over other possible
   emotions. No emotion, no feeling is either good or
   bad. Those words, good and bad, are NOT feelings.
   Those are adjectives. Improving your feelings

vocabulary, and your feelings IQ is a skill that can be easily learned. The more individuals become competent at feeling, the more competent we will become as a community at honoring feelings and using them as navigational tools towards "love." We're not talking about emotional intelligence, here—which is a skill that is primed by mindfulness. We're simply focusing on feelings as if they were a geography or anatomy quiz. Can you accurately name and understand >75% of your feelings when they occur? If not, this is a practical area you can improve on today.

As Unconventional Communities

1. Renovate Community "Rules."

COMMUNITY "RULES" INVOLVE:

LAWS: Guidelines on what is impermissible and punishable. They are developed to protect us from the worst case scenario

MORALS: Guidelines for what behaviors are "right" and "wrong." Groups (such as families, programs, small businesses, associations) often establish, campaign, and reinforce morals.

ETHICS: Guidelines for what qualities, and associated behaviors, are valued, prioritized, and upheld. They are developed for us to have standards.

Psychologists call these rules "norms." Renovation must occur in all of the three main conventional of social rules. Rules at the Community level tend to be based on our negativity bias—centering focus on what we are against, what we want to prevent or avoid. In fact, most laws are written in this energy and from this perspective. Businesses, that center their practices, and rules, on primarily following the law are allocating most of their resources to the lowest standard of care.

Morals often follow suit, establishing rules for what is acceptable and what is not based on what they fear, want to avoid, or want to stop.

Some professions (communities) have established ethics to drive their shared attention towards the highest ideals of practice. Many ethics, however, are often created out of fear, wanting to prevent/fix/solve something, versus specifically attending to what they want to create or foster.

Communities in and of themselves are both the generators of, the disseminators of, and the judges of our shared rules/norms. To attend to love requires that these rules/norms are renovated to generate trust, harmony, gratitude, pleasure and joy.

EXAMPLES OF HOW COMMUNITIES HAVE SHIFTED THEIR RULES

Parenting: Research shows that 50% of parents these days report actively taking a different approach to their role compared with their own upbringing. The #1 area that they want to shift? Yep, you guessed it: they deliberately want to focus on love and the quality their relationship with their children more.

Education: Policies, morals, ethics and norms for early childhood education have seen a dramatic shift in the last 15 years. More and more schools are favoring prosocial skills (kindness campaigns), down playing grades and competition, and prioritizing play in the learning environment.

Organizations: Renovation of rules around sick and personal leave have occurred in 17% of corporations since 2020. One fun trend I've seen is how more and more companies shut down during the same weeks in the year (in winter, spring and summer) to systemically foster the conditions of rest and peace. A lot of organizational research has shown that vacation stress impedes the ability of workers to recover and rejuvenate. When you're on leave, but all the rest of your team is not, fear of getting behind or losing productivity dominates your attention.

2. Incentivize actions of "love."

People and groups sometimes (strangely) get punished for not following the laws, or morals, or ethics of that respective system. More and more communities, such as the legal system, will soon focus on prevention of crime versus punishment.

 IN

HOW CAN COMMUNITIES HELP US TO ATTEND TO LOVE BETTER?

LISTEN TO EXECUTIVE COACH JERRY HAACK FROM PRIMAL LEADERSHIP ANSWER THIS CHECK IN.

Currently, groups and communities still tend not to get rewarded, tangibly, by or as a community for upholding standards of "generating pleasure, trust, gratitude, joy and peace." Many Communities espouse that they value peace or they value joy. And of course, they do. We all do. Still, most groups, businesses and communities prioritize other things **over** these feelings and values.   We need awards for businesses and communities that measure and perform well in those shared emotions. Not as the means to generate capital, as the result in and of themselves.

3.   Spread Love as a skill.

While messages and stories of love are necessary force of good our society, they are not sufficient to alter our attention. Communities that intend on cultivating either more "peace" or more "joy" (the dual pathways towards love) need to identify the specific social skills that foster those states. A few ways communities can do this.

- Favor compassion training over empathy building. Some research shows that empathy, or feeling the pain of someone, often leads to emotional overwhelm, negative/anxious e, and distress. Empathy often provokes one person to attune to, or conform to, the other person's mindset, heart set or preferred actions. Instead of connecting completely, and merging with them, compassion involves a degree of detachment, while giving others warmth and care. When research Compared two training programs, empathy training versus compassion training, the brains of individuals that learned primarily how to be compassionate tended to generate more dopamine, positive emotions and a greater tendency for prosociality.

- Reduce use, and a public preference for hate/fear language. The awesome research team at Stanford have developed a dictionary that identifies, codifying and analyzes the degree to which language is leveraged to produce hear, aggression, and many feelings away from those on the love pathway (17). They have analyzed just how much "hate" language each past president has used Soon, we can use technology like this to provide data on social media language, political candidate language, leaders and followers language, and even group and team language. Think of how we use and enjoy sports these days. Applying a game like approach to spreading more "love language" in various will be very fun (or loving!) to experience.

Conclusion

This is it. It is happening. We clearly can pave the way for love over fear. To attend to it, to redefine it, and to replicate it in mass market over other stories. I believe you are already playing a role in this game, and I believe you are ready for more love.

The Bright Ideas of Us

Check In: How can communities help us attend to love better?

"A few years after kids take sex education, they should be required to take a class on love education. It can inform them on the skills necessary for basic relationships to foster trust, and pleasure."

---Grocery Store Clerks, Publix off of Gandy and Himes

I ASKED SEVERAL PEOPLE I RESPECT TO ANSWER THIS
WHOLISTIC QUESTION. NONE OF THEM KNEW WHAT THE
OTHERS SHARED...

See a pattern here?

IF BY 2029, MORE THAN 35% OF OUR GLOBAL
COMMUNITIES ADOPTED ONE SKILL OR
ACHIEVED ONE MAJOR SHIFT IN HOW THEY
OPERATE, WHAT WOULD LEAD TO
GREATEST PROSOCIAL IMPACT?

WE LIVE IN A WORLD WHERE COMMUNITIES ARE CRUMBLING AS A
RESULT OF OUR ONGOING DISCONNECTION AS PEOPLE, CULTURES,
AND WORLDS. MORE AND MORE OFTEN PEOPLE FEEL A DEEP SENSE OF
LONELINESS IN THEIR LIFE, AND THEY ARE STARVING FOR CONNECTION
AND COMMUNITY. IN ORDER TO GET BACK IN COMMUNITY WE NEED
TO FIND OUR WAY BACK TO EACH OTHER, AND THE SUREST PATH TO
CONNECTION AND COMMUNITY IS CURIOSITY. EMBRACING,
NURTURING, AND MODELING CURIOSITY WITH EACH OTHER AND
AMONG EACH OTHER. TO STOP TALKING AND TELLING AND START
LISTENING AND EXPLORING. TO SHIFT FROM DISTRACTION TO
PRESENCE. TO EMBRACE THE TRUTH THAT WE'RE ALWAYS JUST ONE
MORE QUESTION AWAY FROM FINDING COMMON GROUND, FROM
UNDERSTANDING, FROM EMPATHY, FROM CONNECTION. IN THIS OFTEN
LONELY AND DIVIDED WORLD, PERHAPS CONNECTION IS THE ONLY
THING THAT WILL SAVE US.

Jeff Nischwitz
Chief Snow Globe Shaker
www.nischwitzgroup.com

"FOR THE MAJORITY OF MY CAREER, I HAVE BEEN TRYING TO HELP PEOPLE START THINGS AND IN TURN, NURTURING THE NETWORKS THAT IMPLICITLY EMERGE. I HAVE BEEN ESPECIALLY INTERESTED IN SUPPORTING AND NETWORKING PEOPLE ENGAGED IN SOCIAL ENTERPRISE; FOLKS WITH A HEART TO SEE THE WORLD IMPROVE IN SOME SMALL WAY AND IN THE SERVICE OF SOME PARTICULAR CAUSE. FOR 12 YEARS I RAN AN INCUBATOR/ACCELERATOR FOR PEOPLE WITH THESE KINDS OF DREAMS. MOST OF WHAT WE DID WAS GIVE PERMISSION AND TOOLS TO HELP PEOPLE CHASE THEIR COMPASSIONATE CALLING; TO BUILD NEW MINISTRIES, CHARITIES, AND NONPROFITS FOR THE GOOD OF SOME PEOPLE, PLACE OR AREA OF CONCERN.

IN THAT WORK, WE WERE ALMOST TOTALLY FOCUSED ON ZERO TO ONE. WE WERE TRYING TO FAN INTO FLAME THE ENTREPRENEURIAL SPIRIT THAT IS ALIVE AND WELL IN THE CREATOR ECONOMY. THE RELATIONSHIPS BETWEEN THE CHURCHES, AGENCIES, AND NONPROFITS THAT EMERGED, WERE RICH AND REWARDING. ENTREPRENEURS, ESPECIALLY SOCIAL ENTREPRENEURS, GET EACH OTHER. THEY ARE BONDED TOGETHER BY THEIR SHARED EXPERIENCE AND THE LESSONS OF FAILURE THAT COME WITH IT. STILL, IN THE RICHNESS OF THAT CREATIVE ENVIRONMENT, I GAVE VERY LITTLE THOUGHT TO COLLABORATION.

SURE, SOME OF THESE ORGANIZATIONS FOUND NATURAL AND OBVIOUS OVERLAP. WHETHER THROUGH COMMON CAUSE OR JUST FINDING SERVICES THEIR PEOPLE NEEDED, BUT OTHERS PROVIDED, THEY WERE QUIETLY BUILDING DOZENS OF MICRO COLLABORATIONS. STILL, I SAW THAT AS AN ANCILLARY BENEFIT TO A STRONG NETWORK, NOT A GOAL IN ITSELF. BUT AFTER NEARLY TWO DECADES OF WATCHING THESE ORGANIZATIONS TRY TO MEET SERIOUS AND INTRACTABLE NEEDS, THE CONCLUSION YOU FINALLY COME TO (IF YOU MAKE IT THAT FAR) IS THAT THEY WILL NEVER BE ABLE TO DO IT ALONE.

THE AMBITION, ENERGY, HOPE, AND EVEN HUBRIS OF THE ENTREPRENEUR TENDS TO BELIEVE THAT YOUR NEW ORGANIZATION IS GOING TO BE THE ONE TO FINALLY SOLVE THE PROBLEM. BUT THE POWERFUL FORCES OF TIME AND HUMAN BROKENNESS WILL EVENTUALLY DISAVOW YOU OF THAT NOTION. YOU WERE NEVER GOING TO CHANGE MUCH ALONE. WHAT CAN COME TO US AS A FEELING OF FUTILITY CAN BE REIMAGINED WHEN WE SHIFT OUR STRATEGIC THINKING TOWARD THE MULTIPLYING POWER OF COLLABORATION. IN OTHER WORDS, AS LONG AS WE STAY IN OUR SILOS, WE ARE RIGHT TO FEEL LIKE IT IS ALL FUTILE. BECAUSE IT IS. BUT IF WE ARE WILLING TO SET ASIDE OUR EGOS AND OUR LOGOS FOR THE CAUSE AND COME TO THE TABLE OF COLLABORATION, THE STILL DAUNTING CHALLENGE IS MET WITH A NEW AND REASONABLE HOPE."

**EXCERPT From *Five Keys to Cross Organizational Collaboration.*
Brian Sanders**

"THERE'S NOTHING MORE POWERFUL THAN HAVING A SOCIAL INNOVATION MINDSET WHEN STRIVING TO IGNITE AND SUSTAIN COMMUNITY CHANGE. STRONG RELATIONSHIPS, UNDERSTANDING HOW TO COLLABORATE, AND HAVING THE ABILITY TO REALLY HEAR AND APPRECIATE OTHERS ARE SURELY ESSENTIAL IN YIELDING A HEALTHIER SOCIETY, BUT HAVING MORE PEOPLE WITH AN OPENNESS AND CAPACITY TO LEARN NEW THINGS, TRY NEW STRATEGIES, AND EXPLORE NEW SOLUTIONS WILL BE INSTRUMENTAL IN ENABLING COMMUNITIES TO RISE ABOVE THE STATUS QUO."

**Mark Gesner, Ph.D.
The Maureen and Douglas Cohn Executive
Director of the Tampa JCCs
Home | Shanna and Bryan Glazer JCC**

PERHAPS IRONIC, GIVEN THE FRAMING OF THE QUESTION, BUT A CRITICAL SHIFT WE NEED IS TOWARDS SYSTEMS THINKING, SEEING T[] INTERCONNECTED NATURE OF OUR COMMUNITIES. THE META-CRISI[] HAS MANY SYMPTOMS THAT MANIFEST ACROSS ALL SCALES (ENVIRONMENTAL, SOCIAL, SPIRITUAL, PHYSICAL) AND THE CLOSEST ROOT THAT I CAN FIND IS DISCONNECTION FROM NATURE AND EAC[] OTHER. WHEN WE REDUCE OUR "FIGHT" TO THE BIGGEST CHALLEN[] (WHETHER THAT IS CARBON POLLUTION, RACISM, POVERTY, OR WHATEVER ELSE), WE OFTEN MISS THE INTERCONNECTEDNESS THAT CAN BE BUILT IN COMMUNITY TO CREATE A MORE BEAUTIFUL WORL[] WHERE ALL LIFE CAN THRIVE.

Caleb Quaid
Founder, Regenerative Shift
Regenerativeshift.com

COLLABORATION HAS THE SINGLE BIGGEST IMPACT ON ANY SOCIETY, GROUP, OR ORGANIZATION. AND I MEAN TRUE COLLABORATION FOR POSITIVE CHANGE THAT REACHES ACROS[] TYPICALLY DIVIDED SPECTRUMS LIKE POLITICS, RELIGION, RAC[] ETHNICITY, GENDER, AGE, INCOME, AND OTHER SOCIETAL WALL[] WHEN WE SEE THE ACTUAL POWER OF WHAT LIFTING, SOLVING, ENDURING, AND FOCUSING TOGETHER CAN ACHIEVE WE CREATE TSUNAMI AND AMPLIFICATION OF SOCIETAL IMPACT AND EMPATHY THAT BECOMES MORE POWERFUL THAN THE DIVISIVE FORCES WHICH PREY UPON CHAOS AND DISUNITY.

Roger Curlin
Executive Director of the EDGE
Business District Association
director@edgedistrict.org

DISCOVERING

HOW TO

Have

ME

and

YOU'RE

HOLD

ALL OF

YOURSELF

too

Radical INVITATION

Name a few invitations you are receiving right now. Include both inner ones, and outer ones.

CHAPTER 6

our connection is a radical invitation

Towards Diversified Power, Away from Zero Sum Relating

"It's my way or the highway."

I had a fight once where I ended up making a decision to walk on the side of a mountain highway rather than conform to the rules of the driver.

I was between the ages of 9 to 12 and stubborn.

My adversary was over the age of 40 and stubborn.

Not only was my decision childish, and potentially dangerous, it reflected a major norm of being in relationships today: you have to pick a side, and usually there's only one way to win.

One person's perspective of reality, one person's preferences, one person's needs, goals, wounds and wishes dominate others. The "others" must stay and either cope, coalesce, adapt, conform, OR face either rejection, punishment or judgement. The other alternatives are rebellion or leaving.

In our society, very few groups foster both self-honoring and group belonging. When differences of opinion, needs, skills, timing and attitudes emerge, most people can't "have themselves" and hold onto the relationship, too.

We become imprinted with a zero-sum mindset from an early age. We reinforce this pattern often without our consent, consideration or consciousness.

I'm not a child anymore.

Despite my age and my training, I still find myself in communities, groups and dyads where someone defaults to a polarized position. Heck, at least once a week, that some "one" is me. A few times a month, different parts of myself duke out a decision where only one part is permitted to win. Will it be the part of me that craves quiet, unsocial reprieve? Or the part of me that thrives in playing with the variety of a crowd?

It is a childish way to be in relationship with myself or anyone. It's not only limiting, but also painful. And for the record, that pattern is "normal."

Unlearning the lesson that power is scarce is one of the most arduous tasks of leadership today.

WE LIVE IN A SOCIETY WHERE WE DO POLITICS LIKE WE DO FOOTBALL, CONFUSE CONSUMERISM WITH ENGAGEMENT, AND REVERT TO CONFORMITY OR REBELLION WHEN WE EXPERIENCE DIFFERENCES.

WE CONSIDER OURSELVES EITHER A TEAM PLAYER OR A LONE WOLF, A FAMILY GUY OR A SINGLE LADY, A RECOVERING CO-DEPENDENT OR A STAUNCH INDEPENDENT, A PEOPLE PLEASER OR SELFISH.

We need bad guys to define how to be good.

I'M JUST NOT CUT OUT FOR THIS.

MAYBE YOU DON'T BELIEVE YOU ARE, EITHER.

MAYBE YOU'RE READY TO INNOVATE OUR SOCIAL SYSTEM.

MAYBE YOU'RE READY TO INTERACT MORE ADEPTLY WITH OTHERS WHO AREN'T AS READY, TOO.

THAT'S UNCONVENTIONAL COMMUNITY.

Dichotomous Relating

Relationships in our current communities follow very specific, and yet very diverse, paradigms. Every individual out there is walking around with different ideas of what "good relationships" look like.

Which is really, really kinda cool.

It's also doesn't *feel that cool in real life.* Our communities do not set us up to have relationships that accommodate individuality. They perpetuate models that everyone must squeeze themselves into. Some people absolutely achieve this state—they find or manufacture a social model that fits their specific needs and desires and values perfectly. Many people, however, struggle their entire lives to find or create relationship dynamics where they don't have to give up something essential about themselves OR they don't require

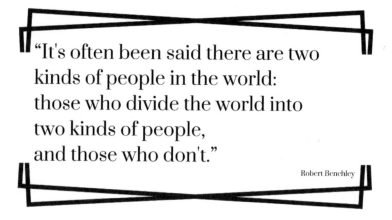

"It's often been said there are two kinds of people in the world: those who divide the world into two kinds of people, and those who don't."

Robert Benchley

others to sacrifice themselves either.

It's my belief that current communities set us up to have more of the first kinds of people in the world, not the second.

Ha ha ha. I absolutely see how my statement above is quite ironic.

Let's explore just exactly how, and why, our communities unconsciously reinforce "this or that" or "us vs them" dynamics. Here are some very clear examples that can help us readily see how prevalent this social dynamic is:

Entertainment (especially movies)

An "us versus them" dynamic dominates, almost all storylines. Here are some examples:

- It's (hu)man versus nature, (hu)man versus alien, (hu)man versus family, (hu)man versus the government, (hu)man versus his former friend/lover/partner now turned enemy, (hu)man versus technology, (hu)man versus the evil or "shadow" side of him.

- Good guys vs bad guys (and the fall of the once good guy into a bad one, or the redemption of a bad one into a good one) is touched on or the central theme of at least ¼ entertainment stories in the modern era. I am positive you can turn on the channel/medium of your choice and easily find at least 5 movies involving Nazi's being dramatized as the "enemy." Modern society has collectively agreed those guys were bad guys. The entertainment industry has capitalized on this collective perspective, and made it easy for us to watch that group in particular get killed over and over again.

- Many entertainment stories craft narratives where individuals or groups are depicted in ways that make them less likeable, desirable and approachable. Therefore, making them quite easy to "vote" or "root" against.

- Groups and communities reinforce (time and time again) who the cool kids are, who the safe people are, who the friends are, who the outsiders are, who the "haves and have nots" are, who the losers are. There are numerous films where these themes are amplified, questioned and/or turned around.

WHAT GROUP ARE YOU PROUD TO BELONG TO?

WHAT ARE THE WAYS THIS GROUP DESIGNATES BELONGING?

Language

Language itself is a tool that organizes relationships. What began as a function of team performance soon became one of tribal belonging. It's important to note that language is not relegated to word or body use, only. Sounds and symbols are also a form of language. Flags are a function of tribal belonging, logos are a function of tribal belonging, fashion is a function of tribal belonging, logos are a sign of tribal belonging, chants or prayers or songs or hums are a sign of tribal belonging, and of course any status symbol is a sign of functional tribal belonging.

All these are visible markers of defining a particular culture. They are the physical tangible expressive manifestations of a community's "US-ness".

Physical/Environmental Design

Our communities are physically designed to unconsciously reinforce "us versus them" thinking. Just consider how most western neighborhoods are designed. Typically, they involve a row of houses on a straight-lined street. One house looks over a street to see another house **on the other side**, one apartment's windows and doors face a wall, outside, or another apartment (18).

Educational Design

The dominating design of our physical dwellings, straight lines, mirrors the arrangement most western children learn in their early childhood education—a preferences for rows. Most educated children were taught how to arrange themselves in a straight line, one human leading another human, in order to get from point A to point B.

This type of arrangement mirrors our hierarchical thinking: one person is ahead, one person is behind. Developmentally speaking, as our minds begin to process how the world works, they also process where we fit *into* the world. Society arbitrarily sets us up to create very intricate lists of the "ahead of" and the "behinds".

Want an eye opening 2 minute exercise?

CREATE TWO LISTS...
WHERE DO YOU THINK
YOU ARE "AHEAD" OF
OTHERS?
&
WHERE DO YOU THINK
YOU MAY BE "BEHIND"?

In addition, many people naturally conjure up straight lines of desks when they think of "how classrooms" are designed. We operate most learning environment in rows and boxes (19).

Workplace Design

Many traditional workplaces also adopted this row-like, or box-like symmetrical design. Even many open workspaces often are designed around rows or boxes.

Not only that, re-designs to make workplaces "more collaborative" often fail to accomplish that goals; (and often aren't motivated with collaboration as a goal in the first place). Let's spend some time examining the open-office phenomenon of the early 2000s to highlight this point.

Impressive research conducted by measuring interactions via sensors (versus self-report) pre and post shift, indicated that when multiple firms (across different industries) switched to open offices, face-to-face interactions fell by 70% (20).

Research regarding work place behavior indicates that when teams shifted to open floor plans, the new arrangement did not significantly shift an individual's pre-existing patters. Staff who preferred synchronized communication (e.g. meetings, ad-hoc interactions) as well as those who preferred asynchronized communication (e.g. text, emails, audio messages) **both** continued to use their preferred methods following the re-arrangement(20).

Although "shared space" is a great idea in theory, it often does not lead to more collaboration or positive energy. Some industries, and teams perform better and enjoy open offices better than others. Some core tasks are completed more efficiently and enjoyably in closed, separated or remote spaces. Not only that, when an organization allows people to choose the spaces that best meet their individual needs, the relational dynamic mirrors those exhibited in remote teams (21).

Organizational and workplace leaders can't simply redesign physical arrangements based on ideals or based on staff requests. Some teams perform worse when interacting with other teams too much. (20) Departments that heavily rely on one another often perform better when they are co-located (21). Some individuals, at least some of the time, require uninterrupted scheduled blocks to produce efficiently. Pre-covid research from 2008 to 2012 found that remote workers communicated nearly 80% less about their assignments than co-located team members did. The #1 implication is that projects are better served at the end of their milestones when those involved in the successful completion are co-located, or when communication channels support consistent, spontaneous and quick responding feedback (20).

The bottom line: our workspaces often set us up for either "this" or "that" configurations. Most organizations, teams and individual think they have to choose between either open air, stimulating, potentially distracting "collaborative" spaces or closed off, separate, quiet spaces. How we create and utilize space often sets up individuals to resort to "us" vs "them" dynamics too—"they get this, we get that" becomes a reinforced perspective.

The bottom line? Decision makers and stakeholders must **consider and center** "community dynamics" as much as they consider individual <u>dynamics. Especial if their goals include creating or optimizing "a well-being culture."</u>

> **TO consider and center a systemic dynamic, in practical terms, means:**
>
> WE THINK ABOUT IT
>
> +WE converse WITH DIVERSE groups about it
>
> + WE PLAN AHEAD TO INCLUDE IT AS A MAIN goal or a MAIN STRATEGY
>
> + WE COLLECT COMMUNITY FEEDBACK about its impact
>
> + WE continually attend and improve it.

Workplace designs that have goals of both collaboration and individual performance must research how their interactions are occurring **right now**, and then also intentionally shift their physical (and social) designs based on gaps and strengths.

Brain Psychology

Now that we've covered how environments set us up to think "it's got to be this way or that; it's Us or it's them," let's peer inside how our own neuronal pathways are designed for dichotomous social thinking.

> ASKING "COMPARED TO WHAT?" is likely going to help you reduce cognitive bias for polarizing/dichotomous thinking.

Our brains, when learning something new, use a process called accommodation. By placing something into a pre-existing "list," we understand what it is, and therefore how to use it to our advantage.

Years ago, I had a mentor who quipped "in comparison to what??" to **many** of my incessant questions or comments.

Our brains often create its perspective of reality based on its quick answer to the "in comparison to what?" question. Sometimes so quickly, we often never involve our "mind" in the process (22).

If you want to become wiser, simply start observing more when and how you compare.

"COMPARED TO WHAT? "

ANYTIME YOU ASK A QUESTION, ADD THIS TO IT. YOU'LL MORE QUICKLY BE ABLE TO UNDERSTAND YOURSELF.

ASKING THIS QUESTION TO OTHERS WILL HELP YOU QUICKLY UNDERSTAND THEM.

Pausing briefly to examine what the results and the consequences of those comparisons are builds your mindset muscles.[21]

---

[21] See resources for how mindfulness can support your ability to expand, and diversify, your mindset capacity.

Accommodation is at the core of how we learn. Learning where we "fit" in and belong is one of the key needs for survival. Our physical survival and the functionality of our early tribes and clans relied on group identification, belonging and performing well together. In today's world, fitting in meets **both** a physical survival need (you can't exist without others!) **and** an emotional survival need.

Belonging is a survival need—it isn't just something that "feels" good. It makes sense that after thousands of years, our innate drive to belong has set us up for power struggles, domination or submission tendencies, and biased hierarchies…not merely at the psychological level.

Neuroscience highlights some interesting findings. Even when we don't *consciously* side with one or the other, our brains do. Our propensity for "us versus them" thinking is so automatic we don't even realize we're doing it. Time and time again, most people default to their unconscious "US" preference on various implicit association tests (23). Other primates do as well. Scientifically sound and impressive experiments confirm that our brains process images within milliseconds based on tiny, almost imperceptible, attentional cues that someone is different than us. We not only like people more, but we treat people better, who share the most **meaningless and imperceptible** traits with us.

The strength of this is most evident when we examine children. Kids show a negative bias by the age of three to four—describing those who are "different" than them as angrier, meaner, and less friendly (24). Even though this is well before an individual can make morally significant, cognitively sound, and physically healthy determinations, a child learns quite early that "difference" is threatening and to be avoided.

Not only that, when we feel positively about someone, or a group based on **meaningful and perceptible traits**, the tendency for "us versus them" becomes *heightened.*

Research shows that the more oxytocin in your system, the more exaggerated your "us versus them" selections become. Oxytocin is a hormone that prompts and fosters trust, cooperation, kindness, and generosity in thinking and action...but ONLY towards people that you consider yours or who belong to a category that you belong to. Research shows that when present, oxytocin promotes less generous, less trustful, less kind actions towards people that you (even unconsciously!) believe do not belong to the same group as you (25).

Strangely, prosocial behavior is blocked <u>until our brains believe</u> that "those" people, the "them" in our lives, have become an "us".

In summary, physical environments, social dynamics and our brains reinforce "Us vs Them" mindsets and relational patterns. This dichotomy naturally fuels a zero-sum dynamic when interacting—both in our Us groups and in those who we label as a "them" (26).

Central Features of Us Vs. Them, At the Community Level

1. Power Trips.

Many people have multiple strategies to obtain "power." Instead of naming well-known methods of power-tripping here, I'll point out one we don't easily see. Group psychology often shows that the person with the least amount of desire to do something, often has the greatest amount of "power" over the process (27.) Just think of how the strange dynamics that get in the way of change, innovation, healthy reform, intimacy, efficiency, when power trips involve "caring less." An example may be helpful here on the above

2. Power Rejection.

Many people adore and requote the belief that "our greatest fear is that we are powerful beyond measure." In very nuanced ways, many individuals and groups reject power as a healthy drive altogether. They believe that it corrupts, it hurts, it gets in the way, and it induces fear. Many people falsely associate power as the source of our fear, rather than examine it more closely. Power is simply energy. Do we fear the sun? No…we fear what the sun will do to us. Our fear is not about power, our fear is that power can hurt. In our dichotomous thinking, power is either "good" or it is "bad." Some of us have been imprinted that it is to be feared.

3. "Us" is a one and done thing.

We think that once we establish a sense of "us" and make a commitment to "us," it's secure. The same thing is true if we achieve a certain title, relationship status, or obtain a certain skill level. We automatically assume it's a "that, not this." We are married, not single. We are a leader, not a follower. We are an owner, not a renter. The truth is that "Us-ness" is a process, and *always in a state of re-establishment.* Every interaction, choice, conversation and moment builds, sustains, or drains an us.

It's important to note that power ebbs and flows exactly the same way.

4. Power is equated with decision making rights.

Many groups don't explicitly inform members of how decisions are made, and leave it up to individual assumption or a "cultural understanding. " In addition, most groups use only one method of decision making. They fail to diversify their decision processes.

Many groups assume that decisions are made according to hierarchical status. With those at the top having the most "decision" making responsibilities versus consciously crafted and clearly agreed upon methods.

People assume that if you make decisions, that means you have more "power." Power is NOT the same thing as who gets to decide what, and by when. Let's not confuse responsibility with power, or autonomy with power. Let's be ruthlessly discerning about this—they all are different motivators, have different brain pathways, and have different expressions within individuals as well as in group dynamics.

In America, and many western societies, we often confuse and arbitrarily cognitively attach power to decision rights. This leads to significant false views of human relationships. For example, do those who vote in elections, who decide how has decision making rights, have more autonomy, more power because they vote?

Calling the shots does not mean you are, or have, the most power or influence in a group.

Calling the shots sometimes (but not always!) means that you are the most responsible for the consequences of that decision. These roles don't have more power than the other parties involved in shaping group dynamics or performance. They simply must live with the responsibility of the consequences on the group more. Still, our current society has many of us believe the false assumption that decision making means power.

5. Unconscious rebellions or conformity are common.

Many entrepreneurs leave their professional positions as staff to start their own businesses due to issues with authority. Distrust of leadership, skepticism or hesitation when others are making decisions, and stubbornness around other people's "power" often are never resolved. Many innovative and intelligent creators, do-gooders, solopreneurs, and awesome proactive citizens never receive intentional development from other humans, or their leadership impact is never formally observed and vetted by other humans.

LISTEN TO

UNCONVEN TIONAL
CITIZENS

Think of all those people who "never had a boss" out there who rarely get the support, feedback and training necessary to improve their group leadership skills.

The result? They tend to do well in self-improvement and even in 1:1 situations. When engaging in broader groups and community collaborations, they often struggle (whether they can see it or they can't) to mature past the "compete for" or "conform to" dynamics groups often resort to. Many awesome "people leaders" never address how people naturally default to them, or unconsciously conform. Many awesome "people leaders" never address why they naturally rebel when someone else is capable of or chosen to make group decisions.

Unconventional citizens. the poem, was written on Christmas morning of 2021, in the middle of a three day silent retreat. It's really the dance between two people or two groups that are fundamentally very different. At their essential core, they have two ways of seeing the world, they have two ways of living, they have two sets of needs, two very different wounds and two different lessons.

Still, they choose to engage each other.[22]

---

[22] If you've read Unconventional Citizens, you might have noticed a series of poems with the word "still" in the middle. These poems convey the inner dialogue of one person choosing to engage another consciously, with shared power.

More than mere engagement, how they connect with one another exemplifies the spirit of diversified power.

Power that is:

Diverse, and respects the diversity

Acknowledged and understood

Shared

Deliberately channeled

Does not require sacrifice or conformity

Not "a given" nor is fixed

Consistently invited

Re-chosen.

Our communities are ready to revolutionize how power is defined, generated, expressed, and organized.

We're witnessing a new way of what it means to be, and have, **power that is shared and power that is diversified**. We can tip the scales towards attending to MORE diversified versions of power, and a power that ebbs and flows, centering on the process more than the product.

Many of us desire communities to shift away from Us Vs. Them, conformity vs rebellion, this or that dynamics.

Many of us realize that we don't know or weren't taught how to collaborate well; many of us don't know how or where to start to share our power, and many of us don't know how to respond when unexpected challenges to those aims inevitably emerge.

Nevertheless, communities need new narratives about power, and new, diverse ways of sharing it.

Here are just a few ways that we can do that:

As An Unconventional Citizen

1. Be skeptical of "them-ism."

Research shows time and time again that the fastest way to "tighten" norms and create group belonging is to focus on a shared enemy. (28). A *few* examples for how this shows up socially: two members of a family/team bonding over problems with another member (scapegoating), two groups bonding to block the goals of another group, the political scene in general!, sports in general, middle school in general, many "churches" and religious groups. Enemies aren't only human, either. People can use the weather, their health, institutions, social movements, social trends and other "things we agree we both don't like" to bond over. Commit to noticing when and how you bond this way.

2. Be skeptical of "Us-ism."

How we respond to each other's pains and pleasures is impacted by our group designations. When we are "an Us", we typically respond to by giving an empathic responses (29, 30) but the sense of "Us" strangely gives us more justification to be less prosocial, less open and less to others, particularly when stressed or in times of conflict. Many "Us" dynamics unconsciously influence, and sometimes overtly require or accept, members to engage in aggressive or violent acts on the behalf of "Us." (31).

In addition, research shows time and time again that the easiest way to justify a certain behavior of an individual is to believe and or say that "it's normal" for people in their Us group (32). Many groups assume that their way of doing things is normal, and that normal means that way is okay.

Finally, there's nothing faster to reduce a sense of belonging than to hold the false impression of, or dole out blanket statements that "we all" are having the same experience, or want or need the same things.

3. Get competent at how decision-making works in each area of your life (e.g. with those you choose to let in, engage, and interact with).

How are decisions made in **each of** the groups that you belong to?

Are the methods for decision making clear? Are they understood by the entire group?

Done by the one with the highest status? With or without input? Done by voice and a vote? Done by a subgroup? Done by full consensus? Decided with full support? [23]

Examine how you're handling group decisions in the groups you belong to. Examine especially group decisions in the groups you are a "part of leadership."

Examine how you react when there are differences, or disagreements in the decisions. Understand your patterns of thinking, feeling and behaving when those situations occur. Do you have any tendencies to conform, to rebel, to compete and/or give up that need your attention?

If so, make an intentional effort to address decision making rights in your life, both at work, and in your personal life. Educate the groups you belong to on how to make this process more conscious and clear. Ask for the groups you belong to for clarity on decision making rights now, and in the future.

---

[23] Check out Conscious Leadership Group for their awesome cartoon graphic that explains different decision making rights.

4. Make diversity a measurement of your well-being.

How well you can diversify your sense of self, your time, your preferences, and your choices often dictates your resiliency during and after situations you cannot predict.

One of the clear ways we can diversify right now with very little effort is to look for ways to express our personal power and purpose outside the jobs and roles that are financially compensated for.

The domain of "how we work" is being radically renovated right now. We are on the cusp of multiple generations (20s, 30s and early 40s) reducing their commitment to a "career." People no longer stay "married" to a single professional identity. It is becoming more and more common for people to be contracted out for a job, versus commit full-time to a single source of income. Often 1099-MISC contractors in the US make slightly more money compared to W2 workers, although gig workers' clearly lag behind employees in terms of health insurance, retirement and long-term savings, and the psychological and resourcing benefits of receiving a stable, reliable paycheck (e.g. receiving a loan, and securing housing often rely on this feature (33).

The gig economy and a "patchwork" model for receiving a living wage are both going to expand in the future.

This feature of community may or may not apply to you specifically right now. Be on the lookout for how it may to someone in a group you belong to in the future.

Nevertheless, if you diversify your mindset regarding how you work, you **will surely discover more ways to express your power than in any paid position.**

An individual's purpose, as well as our collective one, is not equated with a having a "career" or a "family"—our purpose is much larger and bigger than these "boxes", both of which are relatively new social constructs.

Research, examine and solicit the help of experts to fully understand, and double down on, the unique role you play and how you can express your purpose in diverse, powerful ways.

Beyond work, another suggestion for diversifying your self is in examining how agile you are in your thinking, preferences, decision making, and feeling patterns. Do you relate to yourself as THIS and NOT that? (I am punctual, I am running behind). Examine how and where you are you overly committed to a "this" versus "that" dynamic with yourself.

Is there a part of yourself, that is not allowed to speak up, to make decisions, to be acknowledged? If your answer is yes, extending time, resources and power to that specific part is recommended. See the Resource section for places to dig deeper.

5. Reduce Zero Sum mindset and patterns of relating.

This description simply means that we default to roles and goals of either "winning" or a "losing" when differences, disagreements or disruption emerge. A zero-sum mindset is when we believe that when someone gains something, another person must lose something (e.g. think of how our minds work around salaries). A zero-sum mindset says "you give your power away" or someone "takes your power." This style of relating is based on the assumption that power is like an object that is finite in nature.

How do you know when you're playing the zero sum game? When there are only two options: us vs them, me vs you, winner vs loser, right or left, up or down, stay or get out, the high road or the sinful path, the leader or the follower.

Noticing when and how you're in a zero-sum mindset is critical for the transformation of our communities. Why? Because if your main goal is to win, to achieve the result you had in mind, your relationships will suffer in terms of trust, harmony and joy. If your main goal is to lose, to be seen as sacrificial, to give up the result you had in mind, your relationships will suffer in terms of trust, harmony and joy.

Reducing zero-sum, dichotomous relating is a discipline that requires education, training, social support and consistent practice.

How can communities help individuals learn how to diversify power?

"REQUIRE ANY POST-HIGH SCHOOL EDUCATION OR CERTIFICATION TO INCLUDE SERVING IN THE ROLE OF EITHER A REFEREE FOR SPORTS TEAMS, A BOARD MEMBER FOR NON-PROFITS, OR AS A MEDIATOR/JUDGE OF SOME KIND."

THE EXECUTIVE SHAMAN

As Unconventional Communities

1. Offer Radical Renovations of How we "Do Diversity."

Our contemporary understanding of diversity is paltry and thin. Communities that have a diversity mindset invest in measuring beyond what people look like, their lifestyle orientations, or their socio-economic, or other status-based (educational level, home-ownership) demographics. Measurement also includes a diversity of perspectives, motivations, needs and preferences of individuals within groups and between the groups a community contains.

HOW CAN COMMUNITIES REDUCE ZERO-SUM RELATING?

LISTEN TO WILL ROBUS
LINKEDIN.COM/IN/WILLROBUS/

ANSWER THIS CHECK IN.

Diversity also is measured by prolific options for community resources, services, systems and establishments. Research has shown that the more diverse, accessible and affordable these community resources are, the better most groups score on health measures. One awesome example of a holistic community oriented project centered on these goals is the Blue Zone Project. This project analyzes multi-faceted aspects of an individual's health, a community's resources and standards to create a community well-being index. They offer multiple tools, programs, funding and evidence-based guidance to support communities to adopt and sustain diversified health resources.

Communities can also commit to diversifying their own, and group culture, norms and values. Research teams from Standford are working with communities that are primarily "tight" to proactively adopt the strength of "loose" communities, and vice versa. Based on data including 33 different countries, tight cultures are those that have many strong, structured norms and a low tolerance of deviant behavior versus loose ones that have weak, open social norms and a high tolerance of deviant behavior (34). Cultural norms and values do influence individual patterns of relating (35). Communities can honor their tight, structured culture and yet also offer flexibility and tolerance in certain areas. Communities can be inclusive and free flowing, and yet uphold certain disciplines and key rules, following research from organizational psychology (36). Man is evaluating the best processes and methodologies to help communities diversify their cultures right now (37).

6. Proliferate the skill of collaboration, not just give lip service to it.

Communities that create living and working spaces that serve the well-being of their citizens invest in **pragmatic, tangible skills training** in how to collaborate.

If the "Us vs Them" mentality is the social norm, unlearning these tendencies will require evidence based, consistent training over time.

If long-lasting, virtue based friendship requires more than 33 hours over 6 months to develop, why do groups and communities assume that collaboration simply involves sharing a vision and a strategic plan?[24]

COLLABORATION ISN'T AN IDEAL. IT'S A SKILL.

Krystal White

The most critical struggles I've encountered in my work as a leadership psychologist have to do with establishing mutual agreements with others that are authentic, realistic, and progressive. Many people really WANT to collaborate, but don't have the emotional bandwidth for the process, nor

---

[24] See Chapter 7

the available time to do it well. I have struggled with over-committing to projects or possible work requests that weren't viable or energizing from the start. If I could go back and undo things I said no to because I had said yes to the wrong things, I would.

Collaboration isn't a good idea, nor is it an ideal.

It's a skill.

Skills require conscious practice to materialize and become fluently functional. Yoga instructors are required to put in more than 200 hours of study, practice and performance to achieve their certification. Leading a collaborative initiative certainly involves as much complexity as well. It includes mindfulness, philosophical foundations, understanding of social and internal assets, local resources knowledge, self-awareness, emotional intelligence and team dynamics.

Where can we find equivalent training programs for groups or individuals who lead collaborative efforts?

Beyond diverse training programs, communities need a definition of and a measurement for achieving "Collaboration Competency."

This work cannot be relegated solely to corporations and the business sector to proliferate it. If we rely on commerce and the realm of business to promote collaboration, it will wax and wane at the whim of the market, and it will be the citizens at the group level who lose.

7. Widely Accesssible Group Bias Reduction Programs.

More and more programs must be available and proliferated with the chief aim of reducing our individual and group biases. Community programs that effectively get people from different backgrounds with different ideologies to get together, interact more openly, listen more deeply and/or hash it out are rare. To be candid---even organizations with years

> **You are not a kind person. You are a kind person, sometimes.**
>
> **You are not a stubborn person. You are a stubborn person sometimes.**
>
> **We are good listeners... sometimes.**
>
> **Let's end our descriptions of people, including ourselves, with the word**

of repeated feedback and clear integrity breaches involving bias continue to flounder in sustaining effective bias reduction initiatives. Simply: we need more of them, and we need to committ to more of them.

Programs that get two sides to interact, and truly listen to each other's perspectives are needed, but they are insufficient to shift us into a solid sense of "Us."

Research shows that intergroup listening doesn't necessarily mean those groups will get along and become an "Us," especially if it isn't sustained.

Even when it is sustained over time, most groups who interact stay in their Us/Them boxes unless there is intentional oversight in the interaction process (38). Unless the community where they are interacting ensures both groups are equal in size and in treatment, and with a very clear **shared** goal, the divide between groups won't magically fade away.

In addition, communities often utilize retreats or focus groups that bring diverse groups of people together who normally wouldn't interact or get to know each other, often does work to improve prosocial perspectives and "us-ness"…but these results are mostly temporary. If group interaction is not sustained, regression back to the mean occurs. Folks might admit "that [one individual] is cool," but the sentiment isn't extended to that individual's group.

"Programs" aren't real life, and one and done experiences simply aren't sufficient to change our hard wiring. These findings indicate the new programs, processes, and experiential real-world solutions are absolutely necessary to shift the conventional status-quo dynamics.

Conclusion

What if you didn't relate in your relationships and groups from a place of avoiding consequences or winning compliance from others?

What if more of us related in ways that were in our best interest and the best interest of others?

What if that was how most groups generated social power?

I'm not sure what would happen, or how it would happen if those things "happened" at a community level. I am pretty sure that many of us would cry, dance, need new professions.

We can live in a world where the process, the relationship, and the shared energy it creates, takes priority over the "product" or the end result we singularly had in mind. We can live in a world where people hold each other and have themselves too. That world is easier to sustain when both individuals and communities create the conditions to reduce "Us" vs "them" thinking and center shared power that is diversified.

The Bright Ideas of Others

Check In: How can communities help us reduce "this or that" dichotomous mindsets?

"I have seen two overarching characteristics at Grassroots that has created a community that is very much not an "Us vs. Them or This or That" type of mentality.

The first is that the community is VERY open to everyone with any and all backgrounds and/or fields of interest. This helps give new perspectives and avoid bias.

The second is almost the opposite of the first. While being open to *all walks of people* the community cannot be open to *all* people. Some people are energy suckers or super negative. If the community doesn't edit those people out one way or another...the community will suffer.

Sean Suits, Co-Owner, Grassroots Kava House

"We need more Paradoxical Messages. Communities can adopt language that is AND focused. They can adopt policies that are AND focused. They can adopt feelings that are AND focused. We help us rewire our brains from thinking we only have a few options."

Anonymous

Check In: How can communities help us diversify power?

During the last few years, I have been involved in several DEI efforts, events and discussions in my workplace community. While there are lots of well-meaning people involved in diversity and power distribution work, most fail to get really interested and curious about what improving diversity and power distribution means to underrepresented groups and/or specific neighborhood communities.

For every community the needs might be different because of factors unique to them. It could be mistreatment by police/government, or intentional lack of representation at the local government level. If you want to engage with a workplace community, the diversity and power distribution challenges may relate to amount of diversity represented at the leadership levels.

Every community will have it's own list [of what needs addressing and improving]. Unless these factors are discovered, and openly addressed with actions, nothing long lasting will work.

Anonymous

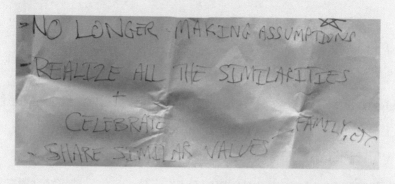

HOW CAN COMMUNITIES HELP US REDUCE US VS THEM DYNAMICS OR POLARIZATION?

GENERATED DURING MAY 18TH BOOK LAUNCH!!8!!

FREE LEADERSHIP INC.

CHAPTER 7

A MILLION MOVING WORDS DO US LITTLE JUSTICE

Towards Friendship As Medicine

So, we've made it this far together. We've covered considerable ground. We've cultivated a nourishing foundation.

We're readily supplied. We're abled minded. We're now willing to address one the elephant in the room of "community-creating." Establishing non-transactional friendships is a more complicated process that we assume. Communities that lack plentiful outlets and processes that prioritize and hone the skill of friendship resort to shallow, politically correct, lip service only, frenemy inducing, or transactional dominating patterns of relating.

Modern adulting within conventional communities makes it extremely arduous and taxing to build, sustain, and dissolve friendships.

As a society we are:

Immature

Ignorant

Incompetent

Intolerant

when it comes to the creative skill of befriending.

Chances are, when you're in a group of people in your community, each person struggles at least in *one* of the areas above.

Even if an individual is a "natural networker"—they can be ignorant of what they 1) really needing/wanting from others 2) their process and 3) their band-with. Alternatively, even if an individual is an observant wallflower---they can easily become more proficient in 1) the skill of initiating hang-outs (aka, here, in this work, as "dates") 2) making the effort to see others despite fearing they'll make a social mistake and 3) widening their band-with. Even the most methodical and impressive of our social role-models can become immature when 1) their feelings are hurt by their peers 2) they hurt their peers and 3) they need more support from their friends than they are currently receiving.

The point here is: don't judge your friendship-ing on your social assumptions of others. We ALL have work to do in being better friends, and better befriending.

WHAT IS REALLY HERE FOR US?

That's a question we all must ask in every relationship we are choosing to engage in. [25]

I'M THE TYPE OF FRIEND WHO...

NAME 3-4 DESCRIPTIONS OF YOURSELF AS A FRIEND

Away from Scarce Socialization towards Medicinal Friendship

Let's unpack our lack of knowledge and our lack of practical prowess to address 1) the current state of friendship 2) what is really there for us when we find, sustain, and compost friendships 3) and how to consciously cultivate conditions where friendships flourish.

---

[25] (re-visit NYP, name your people exercise).

Our modern epidemic of loneliness doesn't bear repeating here. I'm sure, on occasion, you're personally aware that it is **real** and **pervasive** and **persistent.**

So, when you find yourself occasionally "lonely," you're not alone.

At a surface level, let us take a look at why you're lonely:

#1 You spend too much time at home, or on tasks related to adulting.

#2. Are you at home/on a plane/on vacation right now? Reading this? I know you're not adulting right now!!

#3. I'm at home right now writing this. It's occasionally just as lonely.

#4. Maybe we should be having tea together right now versus you reading and me writing.

#5. Sometimes, <u>**OR MANY TIMES**</u>, you and I choose to do other things more than we choose to "make," sustain or compost our friendships.

We do value relationships in our society. We do talk about them as being the most important thing, as well. But our conversations tend to be shallow and achievement oriented around "family." We live in a society where people naturally ask people, especially those in their late 20s and 30s, about when they are going to:

- Get married
- Buy a house
- Have a child
- Get a promotion

We don't naturally ask those that we are close to when they are going to:

- Share more about or introduce you to their new friend
- Focus on making a new (best?) friend
- Expand a friendship beyond its current arrangement (go on a vacation with, or invest in something with a friend)
- Confront/challenge a friend
- Compost a friendship

Yep: that's how we, as a community, "do friendships."

When is the last time someone asked YOU if you were going to do ANY of these things?

Circle the questions that some one asked you in the last 3 years.

Remarkably, for as much talk as there is about community, it's only been recently that more and more people are focusing on friendships. I am positive that in the coming years, there will be more resources on the market and in our personal lives to better understand and proliferate this important role.

We are seeing more movies, TV shows and real world examples of the power of friendship.

WHAT TV SHOW OR MOVIE CENTRALIZES FRIENDSHIP AS A VALUE?
HOW DOES THIS IMPACT YOU?

Basic Friendship Facts

We all have beliefs about friendships, how they work, how they are made, what they do and don't do, and so on. Each of us could write a book, a memoir, a blog post or essay on friendship, extending our own personal advice and offering each other tips on how to improve it. A few in depth extensive resources have recently emerged for us to better understand the facts on friendships, versus solely relying on our own personal theories. While certainly not exhaustive, the resources for this chapter contain some reputable, and reliable, references for digging deeper into understanding this valuable social relationship.

For our purposes here, these key findings from research can provide a quick, simple to understand, broad-brush "state of the union" when it comes to the science of friendships.

It's important for us to understand *some* facts about friendships—and keep updating the facts as we know them.

"WITHOUT OUR DIRECTION

COMMUNITIES WILL OUTSOURCE THEIR FRIENDSHIPS TO THEIR PETS, THEIR POLITICS, OR THEIR PHONES."

Krystal White

Many of us mistakenly assume that friendships happen organically and effortlessly. Research shows they don't. If you think they do, someone took more initiative than you're giving them credit for (43).

THE EXPOSURE EFFECT WORKS WELL WITH FRIENDS:

Mere exposure goes both ways—people will unconsciously like you more as exposure increases, and you'll like them more too. (43)

#1 and #2

Child-rearing and work are the most frequent explanations why people cancel, or don't invest in, their friendships (47).

The Best parts of our friendships: What leads to the largest boosts in our well being?

When our Friends:

1. Attempt to maintain the friendship
2. React positively to positive changes in our lives
3. Offer pragmatic support:
   - instrumental (a helping hand!)
   - emotional TLC
   - cheerleads our autonomy.

Research shows that

Chemistry · Warmth · Intimacy

as being the key building blocks of close, stable friendships (44).

Power Dynamics ◎

·Friendships often play out power dynamics patterns (45). Do you feel more powerful by having friends you feel "you're better than? In most regards? Do you escape power dynamics by feigning that they don't exist in your friendships? Do you keep the peace in order to convince your friends that you're a "good team-player/listener/loyal?" that you're "easy to hang out with?" or that you're cool? Do you play the role of the: 1) devil's advocate 2) the coach/editor/process improver 3) the "I know who you really are" #see-er, or 4) the dependable, "I'll never cancel plans" person? How do you try to prove you have something to offer your friends?

+ THE #1

Having a best friend at work has been shown to be **the greatest contributor** to an staff member's engagement.

+ "I noticed XYZ, what did you think?"

The MOST EFFECTIVE QUESTION TO INITIATE FRIENDLY OPENESS WITH ANY ONE.
Try it on your teenager, your boss, a stranger, some one you're befriending.

+ Easier together

In one study, people judged a hill to be less steep when they were accompanied by a friend compared to when they were alone.

+ Sharing does not equal "Caring"

Intentional confiding in another indicates earned, or given trust. Oversharing often convey that we need to get something off our chest, and any listener will do.

Lovers Vs Friends

Many men 30 years and older report their romantic/life partner plays the role of being their best friend.

This is a relatively new social phenomenon. A few generations ago, people used to expect friendships would be closer than "marriages" because men and women were "too different" to truly understand each other.

19%	of Men	report their best friend is female.
8%	of Women	report their best friend is male
1/5	of men	report having a friend who they can share their life concerns with

HOW WOULD YOUR ANSWERS COMPARE?

INDIVIDUALS, REGARDLESS OF SEX, MAKE FINE DISTINCTIONS BETWEEN BEST, FIRST CLOSEST FRIEND, SECOND CLOSEST FRIEND, OTHER CLOSE FRIENDSHIPS, AND CASUAL FRIENDSHIPS.

Lovers Vs Friends

Both genders report having more in common with best friends than with their lovers.

Lovers Vs Friends

Some women tend to experience more emotional intimacy with their same-sex best friend than with their lover.

2X **one is more likely to die when they don't have and interact with high quality Friends.**

according to an analysis of 308,000 people—a risk factor even greater than the effects of smoking 20 cigarettes per day.

3% of U.S. adults said they did not have **any close** friends in 2010.

12% of U.S. adults said they did not have **any close** friends in 2021.

Here are the Characteristics of Conventional Friendship:

1. Transactional: means-end understanding of friendship obscures the question of whether individuals see their friends as having value in themselves

2. The larger size of a group, the shallow-er our expectations are of others (20)

3. For Fun Only. Conventional friendship today has primarily relegated to the area of pleasure, enjoyment, shared play or relaxation.

4. Poor listenership. Not only do many people report not feeling heard, meeting their unique and subjective needs and expectations to accomplish this aim is a moving target. (21)

5. Don't dig deep. Research shows that most friends don't confront one another when natural upsets happen (22). Other research shows that 4/5 men don't have another person to open up to about their emotional fears, stressors or physical issues.

6. Usurped by romance. Research shows that both men and women often spend less time with friends during the dating phase and first few years of a committed romantic partnership. We often "down-play" the importance of friendship with our romantic partners, as well as our families. Only teenagers explicitly say to their parents that they'd prefer hanging out with their

friends on major holidays. Yet, many adults most likely experience the same inclination. If we show our loyalty, most people unconsciously "default" to romance over friendship.

We can forget about the hype of "best" friends—we're simply, as a community, not even close to being considered "good" in the area of befriending. Many people, including myself, would like our communities, and our conventional society to be more informed, more skilled, and more willing to set the conditions for us to be better friends.

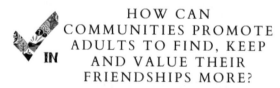

HOW CAN COMMUNITIES PROMOTE ADULTS TO FIND, KEEP AND VALUE THEIR FRIENDSHIPS MORE?

LISTEN TO ASHLEY JOHNSON @EMPOWERPERFORMANCECOACHING ANSWER THIS CHECK IN.

How can we help those conditions? It starts with us educating ourselves more about **How Friendships Work**.

Aristotle's theory about friendship

Written in 350 BCE, Aristotle dedicates two out of the ten sections of <u>Nicomachean Ethics</u> to friendship. He wrote, and widely promoted, that friendship was a necessary and meaningful component of an ethical, and vital, community existence. So much, in fact, that he argued that if people are truly friends, that IS justice, and justice IS a friendly quality.

Aristotle also outlined that friends play different roles for us—some are fun-factors, some are dependable-s and helpers, and some are accepters, guides, and coaches. *

What do I really value about my friendships?

List them out here:

Aristotle's Three "Species" of Friends

Reciprocal Utility

Both you and your friend provide resources, assistance and help to one another

Pleasure

Both you and your friend enjoy each other's company, a shared activity or the pursuit of adventure, relaxation or learning.

Virtue

Both you and your friend provide acceptance of each other, while also motivating each other's growth and excellence.

Pleasure

Virtue

Utility

Eons after Aristotle posited these different roles, research and our own personal lives indicate that friends impact us differently depending **on what we need and what they can offer.** It's a mutual dance, and it's one that must have tactical evidence. For example, the boost friends give us in terms of "utility" happiness doesn't happen unless we report having friends that we describe as being organized, efficient, or clear-headed and *we actually receive help from them* (40).

That same research article showed having friends of virtue (friends who are respected, who are described as being forgiving and understanding, and give life guidance) was associated with boosted scores on both feel good, and doing good, measures of well-being.

Notably, when people had these types of friends, they were also more likely to *perceive themselves* as having a higher degree of personal growth compared to those with less, or no, "virtue friends (40).

How friends make our lives better depends on the QUALITY of the friendship. This is my summary of multiple research describing the different qualities and agreements a friend can provide.

What kind of friend do you need right now?

6 QUALITIES OF FRIENDSHIP

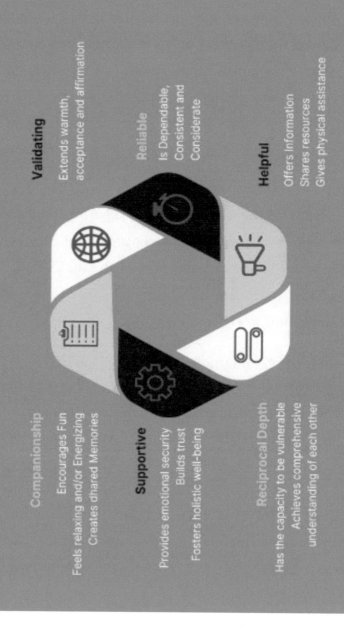

Companionship

Encourages Fun
Feels relaxing and/or Energizing
Creates shared Memories

Validating

Extends warmth,
acceptance and affirmation

Supportive

Provides emotional security
Builds trust
Fosters holistic well-being

Reliable

Is Dependable,
Consistent and
Considerate

Reciprocal Depth

Has the capacity to be vulnerable
Achieves comprehensive
understanding of each other

Helpful

Offers Information
Shares resources
Gives physical assistance

What kind of friend can you be for others ?

What kind of emotion do you wish your friendships would bring to you? (41)

How friends are "made"

What kind or quality of friendship you can offer, and you need, will dictate how much time and what ingredients are necessary to make one.

To find, and benefit from, virtue friends, takes time, and prioritization, and a willingness to develop them. Anyone, and by that that I mean everyone (which is to say, me, I am in this too) can find "better" "quicker" "easier" things to do that to build or sustain a friendship.

One of my mentors* once quipped: It is impossible to achieve something quick, cheap, and good. You can achieve two out of the three, but never all of them. [26]

I'm the type of person who often likes to find loopholes, push the interpretation of things, and find exceptions to the rules. So, since that edict, I've been on the lookout to prove him wrong. Anything that appears to thwart that decree never holds up.

Friendship is one of those things.

---

[26] Are you catching a theme here. Through this book I mention mentors no less than 6 times. Find all references and win a T-shirt.

Most people say they are "friends" when really they are acquaintances. Our psychological HUNGER for friends often attempts to rush the process along, following our society's demand for instant gratification. We are rather ignorant on how involved the process is, and what to do with the time we do have to cultivate *reciprocal* connection vs mere interaction.

Research out of the UK determined that an emotionally sound friendship is quite the involved process. It takes an investment of eleven high quality interactions, lasting around three hours long, extended over a six month period (42). That means—it takes over 2000 hours to "build" a close friend. Two-thirds of those who took part in that research said they were actively looking to add to their inner circle and need a good number of friends to feel content

LISTEN TO
THE FRIEND YOU NEED
IS THE ONE WHO WILL TELL YOU WHEN YOU'RE PLAYING SMALL

The poem, *The friend you need is the one who will tell you that you're playing small*, refers to the type of friendship Aristotle called a Virtue friendship.

It's about reclaiming friendship as a key pillar of a vital life. It's about "saving" friendship, reclaiming the value of friendship, and remembering the cycle of friendship. If a friendship was a high-value social currency, how would we treat it differently?

Maybe the friend you need isn't the one that will expand your spirit. Maybe you have another (human) resource for that! Maybe the friend you need is the one who will comfort you when you're scared. Maybe the kind of friend you need will come move your couch or will take you to the doctor.

There are aspects of this poem that are deeply personal to me, it was the last poem written for Unconventional Citizens and it was shared with my best friend at the time before its publication in winter of 2022. I knew I was going to write one about friendship, and that it needed time and more crafting than the others. All other parts of the book, from the dedication to the acknowledgements, were complete at the time of writing it. At the time, she was the only one who knew that process was intentional on my part.

Why do we sometimes save the best for "last?" What a silly mantra.

Research, and my own personal life revealed to me, that we save many things just for our friends. But we call our friends "just friends." Still, for many people: there are things that friends know about you that your parents/partners/children don't know. There are many things about you that your coworkers don't get, and your neighbors will hardly pick up on.

Your virtue friends love you, regardless, and in a different way. The poem also suggests that there are also things that a friend can point out to you that you hear more openly, more graciously, more carefully, compared to feedback given from any other human source.

The poem suggests that many people talk about friends, or Instagram about friends, or share right cool mantras about friends....when a million words do [friends] little justice.

Friendship is active medicine. Words don't suffice to honor it.

Aristotle argued that virtue friendships last longer because they were founded on the individual's virtuous characteristics, which he saw as relatively unchanging. Research backs this up: having a friend that you friend high on Virtue characteristics is more likely to endure past a season versus a friend that you pursue pleasure with (40).

Today, my friends are the highest, most elevated role in my life. They value, and graciously humor, my constant tending to each other's truth. The beginning and end of the poem pay homage to Check In*, a process that relies on clarifying one's intention and calling on others to share their genuine perspective. If we want something in addition to having fun with our friends (which is VERY valuable!), we must be willing to ask them questions and we must be willing to express our answers. In addition: the fastest way we can accurately measure the impact we have on others ***is to directly ask them*** "how did I do [in relation to my intention?]" and ***for them to share their genuine perspective.***[27]

Friendship Tools.

What people THINK they need to make friends often are misguided assumptions. The things we say are important to share, like similar personalities, worldviews, and hobbies, just don't matter that much. The characteristics we think we need to possess as individuals to start friendships as an adult, like being interesting and well-spoken, aren't as critical as we assume.

The tools you need to use when it comes to making new friends, in order of MOST critical to least critical, are[28]:

---

[27] We at Free Leadership Inc have made friendship raising one of our missions.

[28] ADAPTED FROM SCHAFER'S FORMULA

PROXIMITY: Being physically around others you are friending. You gotta show up either physically or emotionally.

FREQUENCY: You need to sustain consistent interaction with those you are building a friendship with.

DURATION: The longer the interaction, the more opportunity you have to build emotional trust and understanding.

DEPTH: The deeper you go, the more real you get, the more "intense" or "vulnerable" sharing feels. Often, this builds bonds better friend you become.

Look over that list again.

- Which one out of the four comes easily to you when you want to build your friendships?
- When you want to sustain the ones you have?
- Which one out of the four do you need to focus on more than the others?

No really—this is the part where you journal or take a note or something to mark your self-awareness.

If you don't truly answer, how are we going to get better at being better friends?

How can Unconventional Communities use the tools we've covered this far to facilitate us to shift towards friendships as medicine?

As An Unconventional Citizen

1. Commit time, energy, deliberate focus to friendship building, sustaining, and dissolving.

Based on the science, here are some suggested template personal friendship goals:

- sustain 2-3 most important friendships every year
- build a new friend every other year,
- dissolve a friendship every 3 years (43).

Examine the 3 Stages of "Your People." Take 5 minutes and bullet point the initials of people in each stage.

Who are you currently forming/rebuilding a connection with?

Who are you honoring and sustaining positive connections with?

Who are you mourning/composting old patterns with?

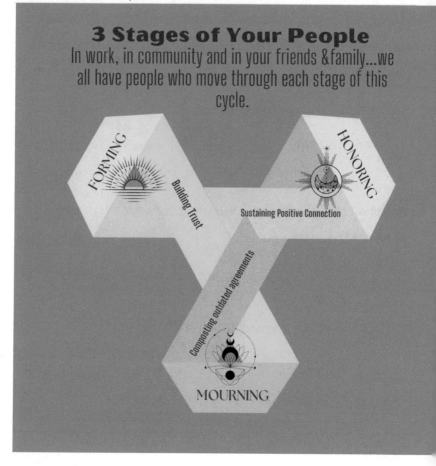

3 Stages of Your People

In work, in community and in your friends & family...we all have people who move through each stage of this cycle.

FORMING

HONORING

Building Trust

Sustaining Positive Connection

Composting outdated agreements

MOURNING

1. Diversify.

If you don't tend to, and deliberately diversify, your involvement in community, your results and OUR results, won't have the cross-pollination power and sustainability that they could.

Diversify WHO you are befriending and HOW you are befriending.

Get Clear on the WHO first:

Step 1: Consider diversity that's "on the outside"---how people look: their sex, their gender, their age, their relational status, their neighborhood, their people.

Step 2: Consider the diversity that's "on the inside"--their orientations. Their relational status and orientations, sexual orientation, political orientations, professional orientations, news orientations, religious/spiritual orientations, environmental orientations…you get the point.

Step 3. Consider the deeper diversity on the inside--- different motivators, preferences, social routines, hobbies, emotional openness and depth, approach to time/money/health management, philosophical conversation, and sharing.

Understanding the four main needs people have, and in what order, is likely helpful if you have difficulty knowing how to identify people's diversity.*

Step 4: Go back to who you named as "Your People." How diverse are they? What level needs more diversity? What is missing? Take note. You can either add that missing element in a current relationship or look for a new relationship, no matter what level they are in, to bring that element into your social sphere.

Get Clear on the How part second:

Remember what we learned earlier; befriending requires consistent "dating." The image on page 205 is how you can diversify how you "date" those you are trying to build or sustain friendship with. Many people find that recipe for dating helpful for intentionally creating diverse "dates" with their children, partner, or teams that they lead as well.

BUILDING FRIENDS BASICS

How to Create Sustainable Social Belonging

MEET

11 different "dates" → each lasting 3 hours long → over 6 months

MADE

DIVERSIFY THE FOCUS OF YOUR "DATES"

learning | conversational | entertainment | project | physical | relaxation

REQUIRES...

Specific Invitations → *Intentional Responses*

"Let's do [X] together, this ..."

"How about [X] after ..."

Shared Prioritization over other free time options

Exchanging more emotionally vulnerable information or experiences at least 20% of the time.

Check In on the 2-3 most important friends you named from your "Name Your People" exercise very other week.

Spend 8-16 hours a month on your friendships.

2. More Willingness to confront.

> Why do we sacrifice our friends for our romantic partners, children or work: We have used up all our "fight" coupons in all other relationships. Real friends generate energy for confrontation.

Studies show we are more likely to avoid problems and hold in anger and other negative emotions with friends than with romantic partners

(45). *One major, and fixable*, reason I believe we sacrifice our friends for our romantic partners, children or work: We have used up all our "fight coupons" in the latter relationships.

All relational research indicates that we achieve commitment only after we consciously choose to tackle our conflicts (46). Real friends generate energy for confrontation. Not simply about behavior that impacts the friendship—friends often are in the best position to confront one another about each other's mis-steps in specific situations, as well as directly addressing how each other's patterns of acting, thinking or feeling might be contributing to issues.

If we want a healthy community, we must confront "what hurts." Confronting a friend about their health behaviors, social habits, mental well-being, and their relational choices is necessary for vitality, long-term commitment, and growth.

Friends who confront you, or you confront, with the each other's best interest in mind, often are more committed to one another, sometimes even when the issue remains unresolved (45).

As Unconventional Communities

1. Invest in programs and initiatives and physical hubs devoted to friendship first (versus a means to another end).

If local communities don't invest in people and programs that efficiently, expertly and with a high level of integrity, who guide us to build social connections, a few savvy **businesses will. They already are.** If an entity's primary goal is to financially profit from a friendship-solution, that's a no thank you for me. We need new ways, and new systems that don't take our social weaknesses and needs and profit off them, leaving citizens overly reliant on them. What do we do with medicine as a society? We professionalize and capitalize on it. Let's ensure that doesn't happen with friendship. Communities can invest in social enterprises and incubators on small scales that ensure that the public well-being is being served over a bank account. This movement is already happening. Non-profits and other social enterprises are renovating into strip malls, old churches and outdoor venues simply for community life offerings that are not attached to any religion/spirituality practice, sports or physical education, or professional trade or social membership club. They are innovating ways to earn revenue to support their spaces and staff. The educational, financial, technological and government communities can partner together to scaffold, accredit/endorse and audit such ventures.

2. Communities can shift the language and narrative use away from " just friends" or "more than friends."

This language suggests that we view friendship as light-hearted and trivial—that friendship doesn't matter, make an impact, as much as it does.

3. Offer parriage, or platonic life bonding.

Communities can expand the idea of marriage beyond romantic pair bonds. Communities who innovate new social dynamics will surely celebrate commitments between friends, whether it is a 1:1 dynamic or within a small groups. Communities can centralize friendship as valuable achievement. Legal rights and tax benefits similar to marriage can be afforded to long-lived friends

3. Continued, Diversified Research.

A lot of friendship science involves college age students, which doesn't exactly translates to those in their 30s and beyond. In addition, a lot of findings were non-existent, sparse, contradictory, fragmentary, and not well replicated. Grassroots research that occurs in a systemic, rigorous and scientific manner can occur outside of educational institutions and beyond personal memoirs. Large corporate organizations can sponsor or host such research goals.

Conclusion

If we are to care better for our community, we must move beyond social habits where we relegate our personal well-being to only a select few people. We need friends outside our romantic partnerships, outside our families, outside our professional pursuits---outside our "groups." One or two people, or one social group, cannot meet all our individual needs. You cannot be your only resource, and two other humans or one hobby isn't designed for it either. We must expand our social resources through the medicine of friendship.

The world needs more from Us.

The Bright Ideas of Others

There are plenty of places where we can network, not many to friend work.

Please answer this "Check In": How can communities help individuals promote adults to find and value friendships more?

"The old way of making friends isn't the new way—and I'm not talking about technology here. I'm not a fan of apps that friend match because really---those apps are there to make money, not make friends, and in a fast way. As a guy, it's easier for me to ask out some one I'm interested in sexually, not socially—and even that is a challenge to me. Didn't you (Krystal) once mention you'd be doing a speed dating event with friends? I'll come if you do. "

-A guy who attends Mindful Men, St Pete.

"Free Leadership runs something called Friendship Factory, where they curate small dinner parties consisting of people from wildly different backgrounds. It's personal, because someone in your "interaction" field invites you. Let's help other communities adopt this simple to execute program."

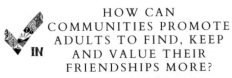

HOW CAN COMMUNITIES PROMOTE ADULTS TO FIND, KEEP AND VALUE THEIR FRIENDSHIPS MORE?

LISTEN TO DAVE
@DAVEATBUILTBYDMC
ANSWER THIS CHECK IN.

HOW CAN COMMUNITIES SPREAD MORE LOVE OVER FOCUSING ON FEAR BASED MESSAGES?

IS NOT

persistence

Sole Proof

LOVE

CHAPTER 8

Doing More Undoes Our Dreams

Towards Enlighted Loss, Away from Ending Aversion

When I was around 10 years old, I surprisingly won a goldfish at a carnival. I played one of those games where you threw one ping pong ball into bowls where the fish were swimming. If you got it in one, you win the fish. When I won, everybody was so surprised; I was so proud.

There's something so weird, and yet so magical, about a kid holding up a plastic bag, ecstatic about its new pet fish inside. That might have been my first memory where I felt my heart might burst.

All smiling, I turned to the adult that was next to me at the time. I'm sure she said many things to me. Today, what's left in my mind, are these words:

"Don't expect it to live long."

You may think that comment was cruel. I've spent little time considering her intention or the perspective that shaped her warning. What I can tell you is this: I believed her.

And, THAT belief did not break my heart. It only motivated me to love that fish as long it was with me.

I really loved that fish. I loved that fish more than playing outside. Ok. I loved that fish as MUCH as I loved playing outside. Ok. Maybe what I felt wasn't love, but connection. I

All I can tell you is this: I have worshipped many common things.

I DID talk to it before I left the house, and I DID greet it when I came home. I DID talk about it incessantly; and I DID pray for it at night before I go to went to bed. I don't believe I would have done any of those things if I didn't believe that I might be gone in the morning.

And one day, it was. This, too, is common.

It's an example of what I call an example of enlighted loss.

That's not a typo: enlighted.

Okay, so…yes, it started out as a typo. During a feedback process I use while writing a book, someone caught it on the book's main overview graphic.

KRYSTAL WHITE | 217

Isn't it supposed to say "enlightened?," he inquired, genuinely unsure.

"I don't believe humanity can truly achieve enlightenment when it comes to death and loss," I responded back…making up something that sounded right on the spot.

So, yes, I made up a word. There's a witness to prove it. It may not stick, and it may not matter all that much in terms of word choice. Everything that's ever lived and dies starts out as an idea, though. And some of them might pull us into a new pattern together.

I think that's what Unconventional Communities all is about.

The word made editing this book a little annoying, ignoring all the red wavy underlines calling it a typo. But isn't that exactly how we treat death?

I can't tell you how long that goldfish lived. I *can* tell you, remembering that it was going to die, brought me more joy.

The only reason we find that combination strange at all is because we live in a society and communities that keep loss, endings and death in the shadows personally, but in the news for numbers. We keep it hidden, darkened and unexplored. We perpetuate confusion, shame, and shock when it comes for us. Our denial of it enables unspeakable actions and patterns to hurry it along in nature, inject it in our relationships with others, tolerate mass dysfunction in our main industries, and be complicit in how suffering is perpetuated in our outer and inner worlds.

We force and keep loss away, we stall it, we weaponize it and we make the next generation oblivious to it.

That's why "lighting up" loss has some realistic juice for me these days. When its themes are present, I want to shed some insight and give sacred space to it.

HOW COMPETENTLY AND CONFIDENTLY AND COMPASSIONATELY DO YOU ALLOW LOSS TO DO ITS THING?
DESCRIBE HOW YOU TYPICALLY HANDLE LOSS.

HOW COMPETENTLY AND CONFIDENTLY AND COMPASSIONATELY DO YOU PROVOKE LOSS TO DO IT THING?

WHO IN YOUR "PEOPLE SPHERE" DO EITHER OR BOT WELL?

WHO SUPPORTS YOU TO BRING MORE LIGHT TO LOS ENDINGS AND DEATH?

We can share more social space with loss, raise our aptitude when it's a part of our reality, and we can honor it more than hate it.

We can create communities where loss is enlighted.

Many of us are ready to let go of how we "do" loss together. We aim to end our social immaturity for how we handle it. Read further if you're ready to dive into the shadows on how conventional communities respond to loss, death and endings now, and how we can enlight it together, NOW.

In a recent interview for a magazine, I was asked to look back at my life and name the top three life skills that were the most critical.

I love answering questions with more questions. So, I inquired; "critical for what?" The interviewer (I can't promise you he wasn't AI lol) responded "for life." You try answering a question like that in front of an audience! Let me tell you, the pressure was on.

Instead of wondering who would really care or benefit from **my** answer versus discovering their own, instead of bantering and delaying the work, I chose to take ample time to find and name the truth. My #2 life skill is really about death:

Allowing, and provoking, loss to do its thing.

Here, in its entirety, is my answer:

ALLOW AND PROVOKE
LOSS TO DO ITS THING

Although loss was literally introduced at my birth, 45 years later, I still consider myself an amateur at it. I consider pledges, agreements, and being "in it" part of my life-blood. One of my proudest work titles was "Chief of Workforce Engagement." Now, I want to center loss more as a valuable, honorable leadership skill.

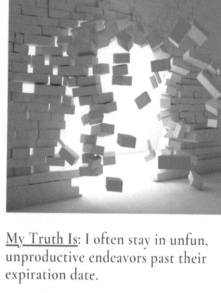

<u>My Truth Is</u>: I often stay in unfun, unproductive endeavors past their expiration date.

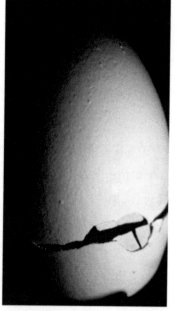

Sometimes, I attempt to work things out that are unworkable. I adore playing hard, working hard, and any feedback associated with engaged investment. I default to attaching to "the thick and thin of it," far more than any alluring hello. Left to my own devices, I have an ego-driven, semi-secret desire to bring back the dead, or infuse what was on its last legs with effervescent energy.

I'm not secure, and often ashamed, about these aspects of my inherited preference for toiling and hidden enslavement. I've wanted to shift into a more accepting, open stance to dissolution for at least half a decade now.

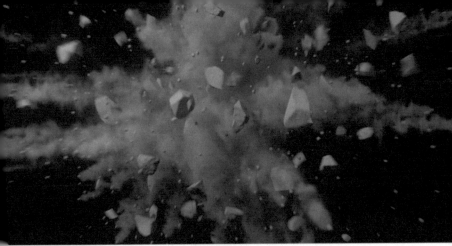

STILL,

I DON'T FEEL OR SEE OUR CULTURE TEACHING THE MASSES THAT LOSS, GOODBYES, LETTING GO OR DEATH AS A NATURAL, POSSIBLY NEUTRAL, PART OF LIFE.

It is.
And it can be.

Disengagement, letting go, saying goodbye and even proactively planning for succession and endings has been the singular, continuous (ha!) most impactful lesson of my leadership journey.

Today, I refuse to equate quality with longevity.

For sure—sometimes when something lasts long, it signals health, vitality, life.

Also, sometimes when things last long, it signals complacency, denial, tolerance for mediocrity and the belief that with enough effort, we can "make everything work well." We are powerful, not omnipotent.

One of the most poignant skills I've learned is to leave people/situations/agreements and also to love people when they do the same, especially with me.

The only quality that supersedes this skill is how to offer, cultivate and resource grace and discipline when I leave, let go, or absolutely break up with a part of myself/identity that I used to love or worked well for me.

Who are the wisdom keepers about loss? I'm admittingly too foolish, to offer any expert guidance. I am looking into and researching who and where the resources are right now. I'm also waiting on your, reader, or a mentor that reaches out to me, to point me in the right direction.

Away from Loss Aversion, towards Enlighted Loss

This chapter addresses our lack of knowledge and our lack of practical prowess to address 1) the inevitability of loss, endings and death 2) how we as community reinforce unhealthy mindsets, feelings and actions when loss and endings are approaching, here, and already occurred and 3) how we can bring more awareness, maturity, and holistic social actions to the loss, ending or death process.

Aversion to Accept the Inevitable

The strange thing about loss is that we rationally "know" that it's gonna come for us. Not just once; it comes for us over and over.

Take for instance, right now. Loss is happening, right now, inside of you. The fact is: 330 billion of your body's cells are being composting today (49). We physically survive based on the fact that death is a required component of the life cycle.

Still, our psychology of loss is the slippery rug that gets pulled out from under us. Once it passes, most of the time, we return to the mindset that we're walking across a stable floor.

Loss is like the trick Lucy keeps playing on Charlie Brown with the football. He knows what's gonna happen, he's had it happen numerous times. Yet, he *still finds himself shocked* and despairing when she pulls the football away.

Just when we are about to feel secure, safe, content, in the right place at the right time, many "irrational" circumstances wobble us. Just after we get the hang of things, or settle into something good, we can start feeling a strange dread that "this can't last." And the fact is, it can't forever.

Despite this reality, many of us agree to hold onto an inherited mindset that "if only we did things right" and "only if we work hard(er)" and "only if this was this way," and/or "if this person/or I changed our ways"—then life would be heaven on earth. Heaven means all the dying's been done. All the loss is over. Happily ever afters have weddings at the end…not widows or divorcees.

….our idealized hierarchy of life over death only makes our loss aversion stronger, and our shadows more scary.

Loss requires equanimity with a growth mindset if we want to grow as a humanity, and individually improve in the game of living well together: If you want a Lucy in your life, it won't help you to hold on desperately to the belief that she'll *always hold that ball.*

She's incapable of that agreement. People **"know"** this reality— they simply live as if they don't. The death of a loved one has been recognized as the greatest life stressor that we face as humans, heading the list of stressful life events compiled by the classic research of Holmes and Rahe(49).

Yet, if any one of us chooses to love another, we implicitly agree to lose them at some point.

I'm not saying Charlie Brown is not a bit foolish for playing that game. Nor am I arguing that Lucy isn't a brat. The point is—many of us are Charlie Brown in how we relate to loss and endings. Many of us easily blame and rage against the Lucys in our lives—for fooling us, for leaving, for setting us up to be hurt by the ending.

These reactions make complete sense because operate in communities where we measure our feelings about loss against immature, overly idealistic and moralistic standards. We feel entitled to prevent losing, morally correct to point out the dysfunction of others as a justification for our loss, and irrationally driven to keep things alive despite the cost or its quality of life.

Not to mention, individuals are easily ashamed when inevitable, and sometimes, un-understandable, loss befalls on us on any given day.

People who are reminded to think about death 5X a day tend to report higher levels of being mindful of the present.

CURIOUS ABOUT DEATH?

Research shows that people who are "in the middle," not denying and not feeling 100% confident about death, still harbor unconscious, repressed fearful thoughts about it.

BLIND EYE

One's cultural, spiritual or religious worldview, and one's self-esteem, often serve a death-denying function. Many people are socialized to "hide" their bodily cycles.

TOLERANCE

The Bonn Longitudinal Study of Aging has shown that the theme of death and dying does not stand in the foreground for older people who are healthy—at least on a conscious level.

LOSS DETECITVES

People tend to crave rational explanations and logical solutions that endings don't always offer. The pain associated it is often exacerbated by trying to backtrack or figure out what went wrong. Most people blame, shame or overly generalize the reasons. We think if only we collected more information, and clues, we'd discern the main culprit.

IT HURTS

Break ups, whether romantic, platonic or professional, have a physiological effect. Our bodies often trigger the release of hormones that can prepare your body to stay and deal with a threat or to run away to safety. It can also trigger a rapid heartbeat or trembling.

IT MOTIVATES

A study of more than 3,000 professional soccer games found that 56 percent of goals were tallied in the second half, and almost 23 percent came in the final 15 minutes of a 90-minute match.

IT INSPIRES

Research has found that thoughts of mortality can lead to decreased militaristic attitudes, better health decisions, increased altruism and helpfulness, and reduced divorce rates.

Let's explore how our social interactions and groups influence us to keep loss, endings and death in our personal and collective shadows.

We Must Hold On!

To Our Possessions and Attachment to THINGS

One social trait you can observe right now in yourself or someone close to you is how we are reinforced to hold on to our "things." Even if some groups that you belong to encourage you to let go, compost, or release things you don't value, use or love anymore….chances are, during the process you're focused on replacing it with something "new" or "improved" (versus bringing light to the loss process in and of itself).

As a species, we instinctively hold onto our physical things far longer than their utilitarian use. The average human being unconsciously attaches ego, or identity, to what they acquire or create. We see this across cultures and across developmental periods. We see this attachment start

> Want to "condition" a person to value something more? Make them believe that you can take it away from them (50).

happening in toddlerhood, where beloved objects must be visible and within reach or a fuss is made. Then the pattern amplifies in childhood, as kids attach to their personal creations or achievements. In adolescence, teens attach to their personal space and creative expression of values, passions, dreams and people. This just dynamic piles on and on until we're adults and all the "stuff" we acquired, selected, created and earned become symbols of "our self."

You already understand the key issue: We falsely believe that the objects that we surround ourselves with somehow say something about who we are today.

They don't.

It is guaranteed that **all of your possessions say** something about who you were in the past.

Some of them have something to do with who you are today.

Very few will have to do with who you are in the future.

It's no accident that many, many people achieve higher levels of insight, creativity and renewable innovation **after** getting rid of many of their beloved possessions (51). They don't let go of their things because they have rejected wealth or abundance, feeling good or pleasurable and beautiful things. Most of the time, they are choosing to create and live from mostly a clean slate and a clean state.

WHAT ARE YOU HOLDING ONTO THAT ISN'T WORKING ANYMORE?

Of course, most of us experience understandable resistance and pain when considering if or how to let go of possessions that remind us of other humans we've loved. Very few people are shown how to navigate letting go memorabilia of people that they they've "let in"[29].

> What percentage of your total personal possessions do you responsibly own and care for *well?*
>
> What percentage of your total shared possessions do you responsibly care for and own well?

This occurs even when those people are still living. Many people hesitate or never "get around to" throwing away photos of others or their groups, despite the nature of their present relationship. Many people don't get rid of birthday cards, personalized gifts, memories of shared vacations, badges or logo marked objects from old jobs, and their school paraphernalia. Many parents agree to keep some physical objects of their children forever.

At a community level—sometimes historical places are preserved for the sake of "keeping the memory alive." Many believe that their physicality ensures that our present and future attention acknowledges the past. Sometimes, those

---

[29] You've Named your People, right? See that chapter!

historical places are beloved. Many times, they sit lonely and unvisited, and strangely are ignored or forgotten despite being part of the "community." Don't assume "historical" means educational either. Many relics of our social or entertainment history (such as movies theaters, bowling alleys, or restaurants) often sit for decades with little progress made for its demolition, or significant overhaul.

> How much space do you need **today** for the things that you'll love, use well? and care for in the future?

Just because something is a part of our history, both those that we want to remember and honor and those we'd rather obliterate, does not indicate that we must make maintain a monument to it. But often, that's exactly what we do.

We live in a society where preserving things is a valuable pursuit, where persistence and endurance is a character trait, where "making things work" floods our narratives.

"MANY OF US HAVE THIS VIEW OF OURSELVES BEING "CAPTAINS OF OUR SHIPS", AND JUST LIKE THE OLD ADAGE, "THE CAPTAIN GOES DOWN WITH HIS SHIP"; WE SIT ON OUR ADAMANT MORAL HIGH HORSES AND WOULD RATHER GO DOWN WITH OUR SHIPS THAN LET GO OF SOMETHING TO GIVE IT, AND OURSELVES, A CHANCE AT SOMETHING BETTER.

BUT, I'M A MERMAID.

WE DON'T GO DOWN WITH SHIPS. WE DON'T TRY TO CONQUER THE OCEAN; WE SWIM AND FLOW WITH THE WAVES. WE SINK THE SHIPS THAT NEED TO BE SUNK, AND WE SAVE THE PEOPLE THAT NEED TO BE SAVED."

C JOY BELL

Let's not resort to dualistic thinking here and assume that I'm arguing against these values. I'm not. Sometimes, however, these values **justify our refusal to acknowledge what is already lost**.

Not to mention, they can obscure our courage and persistence to end things that are past their expiration date. Finally, they thwart our capacity to end things without piling on a lot of complicated blame, shame and grief.

Many of our efforts to historically preserve "things" absolutely do not help us be more willing to lose, bring light to the loss process, or initiate an ending that is full of light.

It's as if we have unconsciously agreed to carry the past into the present...or we have unconsciously agreed not to "lighten up losing." When losing is ONLY associated with heaviness and grief by society, no wonder why we avoid it.

Who wants to consciously put themselves in a state of grief? Yet, that's often what happens. Our physical resistance to let go (of possessions, pursuits, ideas, and emotions) only weighs us down more with shadowed grief.

The Endurism of our Psychological Possessions

Remember how we covered in Chapter 4 that our beliefs, agreements and social dynamics are similar to possessions, in the manner that we either "own" them and take responsibility for caring for them, or we refuse to accept our role.

Yes, we have considerable amount of difficulty letting go of past physical "possessions"—whether they are individual or community in nature. We have **more** challenge proactively ending things we can't see. When we don't "own" the ending process, we never fully process or release the past.

For example, our culture doesn't show many parents how to let go of their perspective that their grown, adult child is no longer "a kid." Our society encourages parents to call them "their kid" regardless of that person's age, their ability to care for themselves or others, or the quality of their current relationship.

"You'll always be my son/daughter—you won't always be my kid," is one of my favorite parent mantras that helps signify that an ending has occurred.

We all live with ghosts.

Very few people learn from their groups they belong to, whether it's their family or their social circles, clubs or teams, on how to let go of old versions of themselves, out-dated ideas about other people, used-to-work-for-us-but-doesn't-now routines for connection.

HOW DO YOU SUPPORT OTHERS IN LETTING GO OF SOMETHING THAT ISN'T "ALIVE" FOR THEM ANYMORE?

I always get a little cheerleader-ish when someone tells me they are cleaning out their computer files or emails or they're deleting apps, subscriptions and other "unseen" and yet present—space takers. I always lean into people who confess that they are stopping a habit, a role, a commitment, an endorsement, a project because their heart isn't alive for it anymore.

Features of Shadowed Loss in Our Conventional Communities

1. Research will tell you that many cultures have removed loss, endings and death from our routine practices. As the agricultural period waned and was replaced by the Industrial era, endings and loss also were replaced by development and technology.

2. Strangely, even if we live in areas where conflict, violence and loss directly dominate individual and group experience, our collective practices around loss are paltry at best. Indirect exposure to violence, conflict and war (eg knowing and ingesting news about wars occurring) doesn't seem to instill groups with adept skill in grieving (58).

3. We've become to believe, <u>over</u> other beliefs, that if we value something, if we use something…we can CHANGE it—into something better

We don't have consistent, repetitive, and disseminated community rituals around loss that opens us up, energizes us, or offers us light.

Not only that, our communities hide, downplay and often ignore loss routinely, preferring to spin the positive plot towards beginnings. Sure, sometimes we mourn unexpected, and intense losses when they occur. It's just that we don't highlight or center many of them socially.

The preference for beginnings versus endings is pronounced:

• We have ribbon cutting ceremonies, honoring new construction. We don't have demolition parties.

- We have weddings, honoring marriage. It's still taboo to have a divorce party and we don't even have a name for the ceremony of that.
- We typically get named once, rarely choosing
- We typically tolerate endings only when we trust a beginning is coming.
- Graduation speeches and parties typically focus on what's ahead, or the hard work of what's behind….not the loss of childhood and innocence.
- We define all the good that comes from endings through the lens of beginnings. Again, this is a cognitive fallacy, as:

Not all beginnings are positive.

And not all endings are negative.

Until we eradicate this duality thinking and communal narrative, we are forever trapped in the cycle of unhealthy, unchecked, "growth at all costs" dynamic. <u>We will proliferate shame for taking part (especially consciously!) of any undoing.</u>

> ONE SOCIAL RITUAL FOR LOSS THAT SPINS A "POSITIVE LIGHT" ABOUT LOSS IS THE RITUAL OF THE TOOTH FAIRY. WE AIM TO HELP CHILDREN TO ENDURE THE PAIN OF GETTING THEIR TEETH PULLED, BY PROMISING THEM A REWARD.

Because we don't have consistent, repetitive and disseminated community rituals around loss or necessary endings, it makes sense that community sets us up to automatically associate loss with pain.

Here are the Characteristics of Shadowed Loss:

1. Loss= Loser

In our modern society, when we think of loss, we often automatically assume someone messed something up in order to have caused the loss, or the loss to have occurred.

That's an example of a faulty generalization cognitive fallacy.*

In sports, often a losing team or player loses completely based on luck versus skill. The gambling industry is based on this fallacy.

Remember, we mentioned cognitive bias and fallacies in Chapter 3.

Loss or endings often don't have any villains. What if there were no bad guys in the game of endings?

Instead of getting curious, our social circles often to go all CSI-esque when things end, but with much less accuracy and skill. We gossiped about who lost what, and often the person "we" determine has the most loss, measured either practically or emotionally. We name people a "victim" if two people are involved; and doll out responsibility for losing if there's just one person.

Many girls and women report this sense of responsibility when experiencing a miscarriage, or menopause, or an "abnormal" period (59). Many athletes, recreational or professional, report this sense of victim or villain, when injured, or they experience less "performance gains" or reduced pleasure or skill level (60).

SOMEONE IS TO BLAME...

AND IT EITHER IS ME OR IT'S YOU!

Just because you lose something doesn't mean you're "a loser."

2. "Terribilize" What Was Lost.

A strange, common phenomenon that occurs when something is lost, and/or something is rejected is that the object, experience, choice, place and even other people are "terriblized." Meaning—individuals and or groups point out, focus on and ruminate on all the negative attributes of the thing lost. Social groups do this all the time in both work and personal situations. A couple breaks up, or a person leaves a work place, or a person decides to end a hobby/passion, and then their friends tell them all the bad things they didn't like about it. One of the coping mechanisms of loss is to convince ourselves, or others, that "we're better off with out it" (52). [30]

3. Romanticize What Lost

The other strange, common phenomenon that occurs is when people or community institutions are lost, most people close to them bring up memories that are glossed over with a veil of positivity. The feeling of nostalgia often is a shadowed feeling, commonly hosting many false perceptions and denial of facts,

Just think about birthdays, holidays and vacations as a child compared to those you experience as an adult. How much of that was fun in the moment, versus fun in memory?

4. Unconfessed Schadenfreude.

Because we don't like to go around publishing or shining a light on how we are losing, we tend to be entertained, secretly enjoying, the loss of others. It helps us feel less insecure about ourselves compared to others.

---

[30] See the model for how people handle rejection in the handouts section to raise your self-awareness.

5.   Death is Taboo.

Conventional loss slices it down to reactive conversations. Speaking about predictive loss, especially one's own death or the death of someone you've let in, is often experienced as a "hard to hear or hold conversation." Many people report that their supportive social circles and loved ones often lose tolerance for conversations regarding ongoing grief or guilt about a loss or ending after six months have past (61). "Why haven't you moved on?" is often a stated or suggested comment, which isn't not only hurtful, it's projective…we say it to others when we don't know how to move on from our own unresolved endings.

LISTEN TO

DO NOT CONFUSE THIS

FOR A POEM ABOUT LOVE

Don't Confuse this for a Love Poem is a poem about a necessary loss, referring to systems, programs, businesses, entire industries and social beliefs that are in a state of demise and disrepair.

The poem underscores that it is our inner knowing, not our rational logic, that must be relied upon and deeply trusted when we are on fault-lines like these. When the places that we once found hope, vitality, joy, trust and well being shift

KrysTal WHite | 242

into places that drain those things, we *know*…and often, we pretend not to know.

Sunk loss fallacy often convinces us that the very place we are trying to make work, or to repair, is the *only source* for our ego's "redemption".

We aren't guaranteed clarity when things need to end, or when they are dying.

And we won't be afforded emotional comfort by collecting all the information before the process starts, or finishes.

We only can believe that on the other side, something good, better, and potentially splendid, will come for us.

It's the promise of religion, it's the product of our wishful thinking, and if we pay attention to how life evolves, it's in our nature.

When we center Loss and Endings:

we make space for what is

not there---

what was,

what will be.

we honor the room that---

is now,

that will soon not be.

Make
SPACE

FOR WHAT IS
not there

Many communities adopt a best-foot-forward culture. This pattern has been widely covered in multiple studies, organizational psychology resources, and community development reports.

The shift to embracing and leading with vulnerability has been not only healing, but also a refreshing movement. Many of us have encountered groups where vulnerabilities and speaking about what we fear, what we'd rather avoid, and what is unpleasant, is not only allowed, but also is a dominant theme and value.

Despite the growing willingness for more individuals and groups to center vulnerability, many groups still do not handle endings and loss well.

In addition, once groups comingle and join together in the arena of a wider community, the social tendency reverts back to a "highlight" dominated pattern.

Communities simply don't or won't foster a willingness to spend a lot of attention (and therefore love ☺) on what we avoid at all cost: LOSS.

I had a mentor once, who in a room full of bright minds and talented, engaged leaders, proclaimed that "LOSER" was the most demeaning and feared title anyone could someone.

Yet, we've all LOST right?

We hate losing so much, that many of us deny, reject or downright reframe our perspective to avoid acknowledging the fact that they lost.

I had a dear friend once break up with me. It took me more than six months to admit to myself that I lost. It took me more than a calendar year to plainly use the phrase "she broke up with me." When another dear friend broke up with me three years later, the exact pattern repeated itself.

I indeed have lost people that I loved, relationships that I loved, places that I loved, possessions that I loved, ideologies that I loved, skills that I have loved.

Were these things perfect? No.

Did I perfectly love them? No.

Neither can un-lose what I lost, however. No amount of spiritual or emotional bypassing can alter that fact.

Despite the reality of this faucet about the school of life, school, very few people, very few groups and zero communities I belonged to even acknowledge that I was a person who lost something. We simply didn't make space for it in the social agreement we unconsciously held onto.

A lot of my pain could have been avoided if we as a community were even a smidge more competent with loss and endings.

What isn't allowed is often relegated to the shadow, where the dark is.

But Loss doesn't have to be dark.

It doesn't have to be hidden.

It doesn't have to be resisted.

Endings belong the bargain of living. No one gets a free ride.

That doesn't mean that they, nor death, need to stay in the dark.

Endings don't go well being hidden. We don't do well resisting them either.

How do Unconventional Communities make the shift towards more enlighted loss?

As an Unconventional Citizen

1. Remind yourself of your own mortality using mindful, contemplative routines and resources.
2. Commit 8 hours this year to educating yourself about endings and loss.

Commit to at least four different occurrences where you share the main take-aways from your personal studies with those around you. [31]

3. Watch out for a tendency to over-ly dramatize or overly sympathize with your people who are allowing, or provoking, an ending.

Watch for a tendency to under-play or gloss over their ending as well. The Loss and endings of others often make us vulnerable, even as witnesses. One of the ways we make the loss of other's more complicated is by piling our own biases, unresolved endings, or timelines onto their process.

4. Commit to exploring resources that help you support someone going through a loss or an ending.

Educate yourself how loss is non-linear. In day-to-day life during bereavement, most people oscillate between focusing on loss-related stressors (e.g., the pain of living without the person) and restoration-related stressors (e.g., engaging in new roles and identities due to the loss), and at other times are simply engaged in everyday life experience. (6) Embracing oscillation and providing mental health first aid to those grieving is a skill that can easily be adopted, practiced, and proliferated in our families, groups and communities.

---

[31] See the Resources Section for many places to dive further into this topic.

5. Suggest that a group you belong to (your family, a learning community, a spiritual or religious group, a committee you're on advising schools, non-profits, or community initiative) to host an annual day bringing focus to loss and endings.

6. Routinely use "The Lights" and Check Out with others.

At least every other day I play a game with people called "highlights." We exchange answers to the prompt: "What was your highlight?" [of the day, today]. Since writing this part of the book, I've become more devoted to WANTING ALL THE LIGHTS, not just the highlights. Now, I'm committing to ending the highlight game, and using "what was your light?" as the prompt instead.

Teams benefit from daily, weekly and project based Check Outs. When someone is leaving the team, doing a ceremony or disengagement process as a team is highly encouraged.

Both are routines that honor endings in a way that doesn't *only* equate them with pain or loss. Instead, it recognizes that by summarizing and naming our key learnings, our biggest takeaways, and **ALL** our lights, we can gain more clarity on what was, and more freedom to create what is next.

As Unconventional Communities

1. Re-vitalize, renovate and/or Reinstate Day of the Dead. There are many cultures that continue to honor this holy period of time. Learning from and leveraging their best practices without dogmatism would shift more light onto the universal part of loss.

2. Name a month for honoring loss, endings, and even death. Run campaigns promoting and incentivizing people to clear and clean out their individual dwellings, and their physical shared spaces. Run campaigns promoting and incentivizing personal and group reflection to name and honor:

    a. What "used to be" and its ending.
    b. Who has lost what?
    c. Open, social acknowledgement.

Imagine if community centers had annual bonfires inviting groups and individuals to come and name their loss and endings in some manner. Imagine if schools held vigils not only for collective acts of violence or shocking loss, but for the losses each individual experienced that year.

3. Endorse, advance and position more death educators and practitioners.

We can honor, invest in and expand the outreach of Death Dulas. In 2019, the National End-of-Life Doula Alliance (NEDA) had 260 members in the U.S.; membership grew to 1,545 doulas as of January 2024. Communities that disseminate this certification and role will surely be the role models for others.

Help others become aware of, and continue to grow the use of dignity therapy. DT is an innovative, brief, and individualized psychotherapy which aims to reduce psychosocial–existential suffering, increase quality of life, and support a sense of meaning, purpose, and dignity amongst people approaching the end of life (53). Imagine if communities centers provided this education to the public, versus keeping only in the realm health care, social care, or elderly care. That's a way to bring death into the center of our shared process versus on the fringes.

Conclusion

We need more than a speech about loss and death as organizations and as communities. We need more than writing a post, a newsletter (or a book!) giving tips on how to "release" and clean/clear. We need more than a "one and done," case by case, unsystematic process. We need more than art, exhibitions, dances, songs and entertainment in general to carry the responsibility of shining a light on death, loss and endings collectively.

We need continuous, tangible, and inspiring systemic role models who establish routine practices centering loss and lighting its healthy, vital and unique role in a sustainable ecosystem, and for us as an evolving humanity.

The world needs more from Us.

The Bright Ideas of Others

Please answer this "Check In": **How can communities help groups light up the loss process?**

"After watching the movie Up, I thought—our kids don't interact with their elderly residents anymore. Death education should be mandatory like sex education. Middle schools can partner with an elder home to do matching programs between kids and residents. Teachers, coaches and parents can attend expert led seminars that year on the loss process." ANOYMOUS

HOW CAN COMMUNITIES HELP US HONOR LOSS, ENDINGS AND DEATH AS CENTRAL TO OUR LIFE?

When faced with loss, endings, and death, my community offers empathy and validation of my loss and the associated feelings, whether those feelings are relief, sadness, emptiness, anger, etc., while also reminding me of the newness to come and stands ready to escort me into a new phase. As someone who moves frequently, I see loss and endings routinely (particularly of relationships and jobs), but reframing my perspective from losses or endings to changes allows me to see opportunity for growth from the [relationship/culture/work life/routine] change.

I honor it with awareness--of what I liked, what I didn't like, what I learned from the relationship/culture/work life/routine that worked or didn't work, what facilitated personal growth and what inhibited it. I share with my community what I learn about my environment and myself within my community. And my community grows with every change.

What a lovely cycle.

CHARLA GEIST. DO MPH
PHYSICIAN. UNITED STATES AIR FORCE
@CHARLA_ABROAD ON IG

FROM FA-LA-LA, UNCONVENTIONAL CITIZENS

Why not

Grant Ourselves Grace?

CUT Or COLOr THESE BOOKMarKS

FRIENDSHIP IS MEDICINE

What is in our best interest?

Trust is the breath of community

FREE LEADERSHIP INC

FREE LEADERSHIP INC

CHAPTER 9

CONCLUSION

We have enough stories, movies, and conversations that point out how lonely, how isolated, how unhealthy, and how stagnant we are as a society.

We have enough evidence that the world is facing numerous crises. We don't need to wade through the data, crunch the numbers, or turn to experts to convince us. If we did, we'd discover that society *has enough programs and professionals* attempting to treat the problems, prevent future issues, and address the root contributors to our shared ailments.

The fact is—we've reached the limit of what the government and professionals CAN, and sometimes are WILLING to do, for our mutual well-being.

What we *don't have enough of* is communities that generate an inspiring and share-worthy mindset, skillset and band-with for co-existing well together. What we don't have enough of are healthy, capable, and engaged citizens who are informed, and who are willing to prioritize creating new community dynamics in *collaborative groups together.*

We CAN become more competent in being inter-dependently responsible for our mutual well-being.

This book here joins many other authors, organizational development consultants, thought leaders and social community planners who urge:

IT'S TIME TO CO-CREATE AND DISSEMINATE A NEW SOCIAL NARRATIVE.

It's also time to renew a value and commitment to social recreation.

It simply comes at the cost of venturing beyond the comforts of our own homes.

Many of you reading this book right now have already embarked on renovating and revolutionizing your own individual narrative. If you've made it thus far, you are well on your way and are deeply committed to a life of self-honoring, sustainable well-being and mindful relationships.

Many individuals also have "woken up," completely adopting new behaviors, new mindsets and new feelings in regard to our consumeristic society, our fast-paced low quality habits, our shallow connections and our unexamined, limiting agreements. Many of you are certified bad-asses in "living your best life." Some of you certify others to do the same. You're committed to ongoing personal enlightenment, relational resiliency and world improvement….not to mention you go on holidays, celebrate your people's key life achievements, and take care of your hygiene.

There is also a plethora of resources manuals, YouTube channels, podcasts, classes, educational series, physical spaces, business and virtual platforms that are all designed with the mission of spreading new ideas and education regarding personal well-being and community building. Many emerging and renovative systems right now ARE DOWN RIGHT INSPIRING. These include:

- organizational workforces revolutionizing intrapreneurship
- grassroots social movements that move beyond polarization, unconventional family systems
- evolving yoga programs in corporations and education
- innovative social clubs that foster fun and depth
- sustainable living initiatives and communities
- social enterprises driving economy and goodwill.

There are no shortages of resources, both locally and globally, with the mission of educating people how to be a better person, or how to be a community.

How exciting of a time!

The idea to, and the call to, change how community works has been going on for the last few decades. Since COVID, more and more of "US" are ready, able and willing to *actually answer* that call. We do not wish to continue with such paltry, shallow and insufficient social dynamics and sparse social capital.

How we *answer* that call must move beyond the confines of our own personal lives, professional roles and family relationships.

To that end, we must double-down on our individual commitment to join groups that boost the social capital of *both ourselves as individuals, and our communities as a whole. We must embark on a new ways of generating social capital.*

Why? Think of all the ways we relied on socializing in order to function just five years ago. Today, we don't have to leave our house to receive groceries, to vote, to exercise, to communicate, or even to earn a living. The individualization of our commerce, our work habits and our physical upkeep has come at the cost of our beneficial social networking.

More so, the main areas where we DO interact the most, aren't the most generative of social capital.

Social capital is the positive product of our social systems (Name Your People! Turn to page 45 to complete your own personal social life inventory). Think of all the knowledge your peers through your life offered you. Think of how your own economic mobility was aided or impeded by someone you interacted with. Think of how many people improve their mental wellness and technical expertise by engaging in some prosocial project or physical exercise together.

Research shows that one of the most powerful benefits of social capital is a sense of belonging and purpose (54).

Social Capital

THE TANGIBLE AND INTERNAL BENEFITS

produced by

HUMAN INTERACTIONS

@freeleadershipinc

Yes, many people report that they just *don't belong* at work. Many people report that they just don't belong at home either. Both our families, and our work teams, appear to be an infrequent people find, or are competent at, cultivating or sustaining belonging "for all" (53). The two main places most of us devote most of our energy go to don't typically feed our belonging!

On the flipside, belonging is mostly discovered and reinforced for us in our social connections <u>outside</u> of these two main areas: our involvement in groups, hobbies and community activities.

Brain research shows the most activation in areas of "belonging" when we are engaging out in the community, not at work or home (61).

A community's social capital can be deduced quite simply:

1) The more people trust, and report that they trust, each other

And 2) the more people who engage in and /belong to groups (recreational, mission oriented or civic driven)

…The more social capital the community generates (54).

Social capital means that people feel good about their relationships, feel good when they think about the groups they belong to, and they feel good about affecting change in the systems that run the community.

People who feel helpless about society or who are consumed by their personal stress, often don't participate in routine, consistent and optional social activities.

Of course, the more income inequality or social polarization, the less social capital a community sustain as well. Research shows that people who live within these low social capital communities act less generous, less cooperative, and less deliberate while playing games simulating social dynamics (55). Individuals and groups in communities with less social capital also are more likely to experience bullying

Evolutionary anthropologist Robin Dunbar's research indicates that if graph the size of the part of your human brain related to executive functioning relative to your physical size, you get Dunbar's #, a prediction of the average size of a cohesive "community" (56).

It's 150 people, BTW.

It is likely that if you returned to the Name Your People exercise that you could name 150 people total across all the levels.

> **What you CAN do:**
> <u>*Vote with your feet.*</u>
> *Physically show up, invest in and engage in social capital creating groups. Most people experience discomfort & uncertainty the first 3 visits to a new group. Unless there is a significant values mis-match, don't base a group on your first visit. If these feelings don't dissipate by your 4th visit, vote with your feet again, and find another group!*

and to punish in antisocial ways (e.g. punishing overly generous people more than those who cheat!) (62).

Evolutionary and brain scientists have posited that primates developed bigger brains, and an evolutionary advantage, simply as a consequence of being part of a tribe. While diet can explain how the cortex got so big, how primates found and sustained a good diet is largely due to their social connection (56, 61). Even today, a nutrient dense water and food supply requires functional social systems. The cortex is the part of the brain associated with executive and problem-solving function. Even today, there is research showing how the cortex growth in early childhood is related to warmth, touch, and "belonging like" attunement practices (61).

Hopefully these descriptions help place into scientific context what's on the line if we don't shift community dynamics. Social extends beyond being a "nice idea" and chasing fluffy social kumbaya ideals. Our evolutionary advantage---our executive functioning, our emotional well-being and our shared humanity is at stake.

Don't succumb to socializing and improving social capital more out of fear, however, rather than "love." Social capital hands down gives us MORE access to awe, gratitude, excitement, joy, and a sense of trust (56) than we'd otherwise have available on our own. The more high quality engagements and interactions you have, the more access you have to those "higher" qualities.

Many of us may believe that finding high quality, diverse, effective groups and communities *who actually practice the concepts* presented in this book is an arduous challenge.

What if we were wrong?

What if more of us believed that communities such as these, both physical and remote, were abundant and readily available?

That is the mission of this book---to shift both your ideas of communities and your willingness to be engaged in them. It aimed to make conscious community life simple to understand, compelling to practice and feel good for us to share.

That's how we will shift the narrative.

- We will know what skills "we as community" need now.
- We will have a starting point on how to master them
- We will commit to actually practice these discipline with our people
- We will readily share our community skills and resources.

And

- We will be bearers of brighter news.

Right here, right now, I ask that you name one thing you're willing to do in the name of our community.

You belong here.

THE WORLD NEEDS MORE FROM US.

This book will only make a difference if you read it, and also you do something with it.

You "own it" (See Discipline #2!).

Maybe all you do with it is to leave it in a tea shop with a note for a stranger to take it. Maybe all you do with it is rip out the affirmations at the back and put them in a birthday card. Maybe all you do with it is use it as a stabilizing force under a table that is a little bit off kilter. Maybe it works well to train your posture.

I don't know if or how you're going to use it! That's one of agreements you sign up for as a writer, and I accept it.

We both need to agree here that it is YOU who will decide if and how, and you who will choose and how you will go further.

CHECK OUT THE LETTER CODE (2023) TO CLEARLY AND QUICKLY GET THE REAL NEED YOU HAVE IN CLOSE RELATIONSHIPS, & HOW TO ADVOCATE FOR THEM TO BE MET

CHAPTER 10

RESOURCES

This section includes just a sample of the resources we believe would deepen your awareness, sharpen your skills or widen your capacity to guide others towards better community building skills.

We aimed to list diverse resources for each section. We included material that provides a basic foundational overview, those that use an esoteric or spiritual lens, those that review and heavily rely on science, those that provide simple tips, and those that are easy to read and uplifting.

Much of the material, approach or language here may not resonate with you. Explore further anyway. Take what works for you. Instead of leaving the rest behind, we suggest that you spend some time with ONE resource here that simply doesn't resonate or isn't easy for you to digest. Why? It is highly likely that someone in a group you belong to WOULD resonate with that approach, lens, language and/or style. By at least exposing and interacting with something "different" than your typical learning preference, you'll tap into the discipline of "Diversified Power" and be more capable of guidance, understanding and/or collaboration with others who see, need, feel, want and approach life differently than you.

Community Systems and Psychology

Tools/Data Focused Resources:

Social Capital Atlas
https://opportunityinsights.org/wp-content/uploads/2022/07/socialcapital_nontech.pdf

Impact of parks on social capital: Chetty, Jackson, Kuchler, Stroebel, et al. *Nature* 2022

Volunteering In America:
AmeriCorps.gov/VolunteeringInAmerica

Blue Zones: Community Wellbeing Index:

https://info.bluezonesproject.com/measurement

Peer Reviewed Research:
Bradshaw T. (2008). The post-place community: Contributions to the debate about the definition of community. *Community Development*, 39, 5–16.

Goodsell T. L., Flaherty J., Brown R. B. (2014). Community as moral proximity: Theorizing community in a global economy.

Books:

Although written almost 25 years ago, this book aptly describes the state of declining social capital today. **The 14 state-level measures of social capital**, along with the Comprehensive Social Capital Index, are described in Table 4 and pp. 290-291, and the underlying sources of these data are given in the end notes to those pages:

Bowling Alone....................................By R. Putnam

With depth, comprehensive research and hope, Tenured Professor at Georgetown University's McDonough School of Business offers case studies and suggestions for us all: *Mastering Community* .... By C Porath

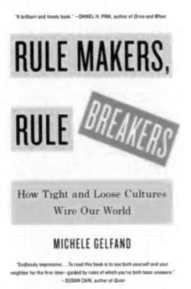

Quickly understand how community culture tends to drive norm development, social rules and defining "right and wrong":
Rule Makers and Rule Breakers........................ By M Gelfand

Connected: The Surprising Power of our Social Networks

...................................…..……....By N Christakis and J Fowler

The best tome on social biology and neuropsychology ever.
Summarizes at least 30% of my Harvard Master's:
Behave.................….............................…..........R. Sapolsky

How this Book Works

Generation Effect (How to actually use materials you read/info
you hear)

Generation Effect | A Simplified Psychology Guide

Naming the Truth

Radical Honesty & Workbook...................By R Blanton

Leadership and Self Deception ....By Arbinger

Mistakes were made (but Not by Me)
...................................….....……..By C. Tavrus and E. Aronson

Check In...................…..............….....…..........By K White

Morning Pages, The Why & How:

https://www.masterclass.com/articles/tips-for-writing-
morning-journal-pages

Mental Health 1ˢᵗ Aid Certification:

Free Leadership.Org & The National Council of Well-Being

Evolve your Brain……by J Dispenza

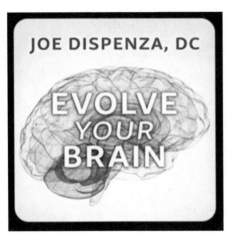

Like Stories of Old—
Radical Honesty:

https://www.youtube.com/
watch?v=6viSZCnIpPY

Social Ownership

Community, the Structure of Belonging

Flawless Consulting……………………..…. Both By P Block

Easy to Read and Pleasing to Look at Handouts for Logistical Fallacies and Cognitive Biases:

The Thinking Shop

https://thethinkingshop.org/

Light read/Word based Manifesto:

Own It..............................……......……….. By D Von Furstenberg

Radical Responsibility................................…….By F Maull

Love More over Fear

Essays on anxiety, society and ideas for shifting:

Anxiety Culture: The New Global State of Human Affairs.........by John P. Allegrante, Ulrich Hoinkes, Michael I. Schapira, and Karen Struve (Out in November 2024)

All About Love.......................................…..By B. Hooks

Best Couples Research and Programs:

The Gottman Institute

Best basic parenting program for love first, then followed by lesson teaching:

Love and Logic....................... ......By F. Cline and J. Fay

Mindset Based: *Taming The Tiger Withing*…..By Thich Nhat Hanh

Brain and attachment based: *Wired for Love* ……….By S. Tatkin

Diversified Power

Mindfulness/Expansive Thinking Based:

Thinking fast, Thinking slow…..…………By D. Kahneman

Society Based: An engaging look at how American politics and media reinforce partisan identity and threaten democracy *Wrong*…………………….by DG Young

Social Relationships Based:

Power, the Infinite Game............. by M Broom and D Klein

Leadership Based: Good to Great (especially the part about the Language of AND........................By J Collins

Jim CollinsConcepts - Genius of the AND

Conscious Leadership Group:

Decision Making Rights

https://conscious.is/video/defining-decision-rights

Friendship is Medicine

Investigative Overview of the role of friends:

Friendship ....By L Denworth

Understand cross disciplined science and the essence of friendship making today:

Friends: Understanding the Power of our Most Important Relationships ....By R Dunbar

Platonic ....By M Franco

The Friendship Doctor & author of *Best Friends Forever* (book about break ups w/friends) ....By I Levine

Modern Friendship.....................................By A Goldfarb

Big Friendship
https://www.bigfriendship.com/

Podcast #360: Understanding Male Friendships
https://www.artofmanliness.com/people/relationships/understanding-male-friendships/

Enlighted Loss

Best Book for understanding loss cycle and inter-personal change:

Transistions ....By W Bridges

Memoir: *The Year Of Magical Thinking*

..........................By J Didion

The Great Divorce....................................By CS Lewis

Spirituality Based:

Letting Go………………………………...…….By D Hawkings

Leadership Based:
Necessary Endings…………………………………..By H Cloud

Attachment Theory Based:
Necessary Losses…………………………………....By J Viorst

Advice Column: Ask Death
https://askdeath.substack.com

We croak Podcast & Leap Community

"Find happiness by contemplating your mortality."

THE EXECUTIVE SHAMAN

The Executive Shaman focuses on enhancing elite leadership and the development of highly reliable cultures and teams. Most leaders or managers never get high-quality training or mentorship before they are expected to be responsible for other people's choices.

It's a weight many cannot bear.

In addition, many leaders and organizations can publicly pronounce or preach about being people-oriented and collaborating and handling conflicts and other DEI standards, but only a select group sustains commendable dynamics for long durations.

It's too easy to be complacent these days.

The leaders, teams and organizations that contract out a TES-led development program get high-powered, highly entertaining group coaching and change management training. We focus on engineering intrapreneurs, and ensuring ego management from seasoned organizational experts. The best part? It's never dull and most people can't help but laugh at themselves with us in the room.

www.theexecutiveshaman.com

We strive to rebrand leadership as a function of quality support versus one of achieved status. We will be part of a movement that centers leadership as a form of connecting people, fostering trust and wise optimism—the modern do gooders of our communities, and the backbone of our collective wellbeing.

We really believe that leaders of our personal lives are our friends, our mentors, and the natural coaches that help us become better humans.

Our 5013c is devoted to finding and empowering people who want to be better friends/need better friends, want to be mindful mentors/need mindful mentors or who want to coach others/who need to be coached. If there was a place and a space that cultivated skill in those roles and then proliferated them through our neighborhoods, we're pretty sure that this would reduce not only mental health issues and conflicts but it would it would FEEL like the world was a better home to live in.

We'd be happier, wiser, less myopic and confused, and we'd have more of a willingness to share resources.

Instead of focusing on conventional solutions of culture development, which start at the top with key leaders in charge of the culture, FLinc's approach is unconventional. We are inciting change within individuals and populations at the neighborhood, and personal relationship level. We target serving grassroots, everyday people who typically support, care for, or serve, others. We want to empower people who naturally like to help others or already are positioned as listeners, to be more effective influencers, leaders, mentors, and coaches.

We aim to improve their willingness and skill in
　　　　rating and thinking systematically. Many do-gooders
　　　　time recreating the wheel or doing everything in-
　　　e, by trial by fire, or by their own grit and personal
　　　ds. They need an easy way and a plan to learn how to
　　uickly coach others toward better health behaviors, how to
　alk about something in a way that garners engagement, who to join forces with (and who to avoid), and how to recycle/upcycle and share processes and resources.

A lot of folks in our local communities care and then launch projects, step out as solopreneurs, or decide to join a board, become community or neighborhood advocates or start a non-profit without very little or no social or business support or mentoring at the start.

Why is it that elite executives perform better? One of the reasons is that they have accumulated "wealth" of a LOT of social support...not simply inherited money management habits. Free Leadership wants to build a bench of mentors and coaches and informed "friends" within specific neighborhoods and districts so that more people can access free, and high-quality social resources.

We at Free Leadership intend to rebrand how we identify our leaders, and what it means to be a leader.

We definitely believe it's outdated primatology to confuse a higher-ranking person as the leader in the group. We also think that just because somebody is going somewhere competently and confidently, doesn't mean we it's in our best interest to follow them.

We believe that 1) who we choose to, and how, we follow and 2) who chooses to, and how he/she/they lead **both** require serious renovation and a revolution in our society.

Our core premise and standard is that the most influential people in our lives are the ones who support us. They often play this role invisibly and often without a lot of credit or value. Think of how our bones support our entire physical system stabilizing and holding us up. They make sturdy possible. Yet their power remains hidden to the eye. Few people go around complimenting or acknowledging the value of each other's bones!

Who are like bones in your life?

We want to find these people. educate and empower these people first to foremost to play this role more openly in our communities.

Then, we want to position them to be more engaged in community at either a civic or neighborhood life level. We actively mentor, coach and friend them to benefit their communities more effectively while also maintaining their own individual well-being.

We RELY on mentors (in the form of board members, partners in other industries who want to launch a program under a collaborative venture, and key volunteers) to be our bones.

Please reach out to krystal@freeleadership.org if you'd like to actively shape our strategy, and/or facilitate a program or design a grant that aligns with our mission to activate invested friends, mentors and coaches informally within YOUR community.

@Free LeaDerSHip Inc

FLINC IS A 5013C THAT GENERATES SOCIAL CAPITAL, AND MORE VISIBLE PROSOCIAL ACTIONS IN CITIZENS AND GROUPS. EVERYTHING WE DO IS INTENDING TO FREE LEADERSHIP FROM ITS TRADITIONAL POSITION OF STATUS, AND REBRAND IT AS A FORM OF INTER-PERSONAL SUPPORT.

CHECK OUT CHECK IN, to master the group process.

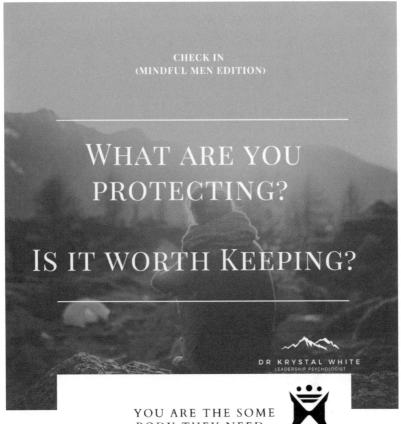

WHY IT MATTERS THAT YOU GET
CERTIFIED IN MENTAL HEALTH
FIRST AID

UnConventional Elements

Deviate

Deviate from convention & status quo stagnation. Use your intuition and emotions to guide how and where you deviate.

DISCERN

Discern with confidence if you're really off/on course & how you are sabatoging relationships.

DISCOVER

Discover what you want, how to ask for it, new ways of relating to others, ideas on how to innovate collaboratively.

DEFY

Defy resistance to change, ending conflicts, attachment to comfort zones, and regression to the mean Practice new ways to let go of the past.

DECIDE

Decide who you are, and how you serve. Use your answers to define your boundaries. Repeat the process when indicated.

DISCOURSE

Dialouge compassionately about social differences without polarization or cognitive biases.

DISAPPOINT

Disappoint others w/o being defensive, inconsiderate, or fake. Deal with your own disappointments & bruised ego.

Unconventional Citizens is a remote learning platform and live peer coaching community. There are over 100 hours of online self-paced material as well as monthly synchronous small groups aimed to improve these skills above. Type The Executive Shaman Unconventional Citizens into a search engine to access.

THE FIRST TIME THE GULF AT SUNSET

SUBMERGED ME

ALL OF MY ALTARS WERE DESTROYED

AI GENERATED IMAGE

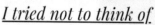

I tried not to think of you.

I'll always be estranged, and you an escape artist.

I've put men in office, hospitals, solitary and the ground.

You still convince yourself you're more dangerous.

when I have no more magic
WITH WILD WORDS,
I'LL STILL SEDUCE YOU

with enigmatic mutenes

AND A TOLERANCE SO EXAPANSIVE
ALL YOUR LIMITS WILL LIE
WHIPLASHED.

with no fuel left over
to reach the blackness that
belongs
only to me.

I'M NO STAR!

but I can take all your darkness
and make it into a cocktail
even mere strangers declare
remarkable.

No crown can convey
WHAT I'VE PAID FOR,
FOUGHT FOR,
LOVED FOR.
why is what you wage for,
still, up for debate?

YOU'RE NO DIFFERENT THAN ME,
ALL OF US
IN THIS KINGDOM,
CRAVING MORE THAN ONE LIFETIME
TO SUCCUMB TO ALL THE
WONDER
WORK
WHISPERS
OF THIS WORLD.

HUMDRUM
KARMA
STILL DROWNS

SURRENDER,
OR TRY TO SWIM TO SHORE

I DO NOT
think of you.

References

Preamble

1. More segregation https://belonging.berkeley.edu/roots-structural-racism
2. More loneliness https://newsroom.thecignagroup.com/loneliness-epidemic-persists-post-pandemic-look
3. Less volunteerism: https://www.barrons.com/articles/volunteerism-dearth-charitable-giving-nonprofits-labor-7df901bb
4. Less civility https://www.reuters.com/legal/government/civility-is-decline-aba-civics-poll-finds-2023-04-27/

How this book works

5. The Pen Is Mightier Than the Keyboard: Advantages of Longhand Over Laptop Note Taking (2014) by Pam Mueller et al. Psychological Science Volume 25, Issue 6.

More Social Responsibility

6. Affective Forecasting: Knowing What to Want". Current Directions (2005). By Tim Wilson, Timothy & Daniel Gilbert in Psychological Science. 14 (3): 131–134.

7. Toward a Psychology of Human Agency: Pathways and Reflections. (2018) By A Bandura In Perspectives on Psychological Science, 13(2), 130-136. https://doi.org/10.1177/1745691617699280.

8. Agency and Identity in the Collective Self. (2022) G Shteynberg, et all. In Personality and Social Psychology Review, 26(1), 35-56. https://doi.org/10.1177/10888683211065921

9. Why free will doesn't exist, according to Robert Sapolsky | New Scientist

10. *How we Decide* By Jonah Lehrer

11. Facial appearance and leader choice in different contexts: Evidence for task contingent selection based on implicit and learned face-behaviour/face-ability associations - ScienceDirect

12. The Look of a Winner | Scientific American

13. The 5 Dysfunctions of a Team: Patrick Leconi

14. What Is... Herd Behaviour in Psychology - Mental Health @ Home (mentalhealthathome.org)

More Love Over Fear

15. How Starbucks Drinks Have Changed Over the Last 10 Years - Business Insider

16. The Letter Code, Krystal J White, PhD

17. Threat Dictionary: Threatening Language Can Be Contagious. This New Tool Tracks Its Spread. | Stanford Graduate School of Business

More Diversified Power

18. Baffoe, G. (2019). Understanding the Neighbourhood Concept and Its Evolution: A Review. Environment and Urbanization ASIA, 10(2), 393-402.
19. The Science of Classroom Design | Edutopia
20. Sensors Tracking human behavior in offices https://dspace.mit.edu/handle/1721.1/62024
21. https://hbr.org/2019/11/the-truth-about-open-offices
22. Thinking Fast and Thinking Slow Daniel Kahneman
23. The evolution of intergroup bias: Perceptions and attitudes in rhesus macaques (2011).. Mahajan et all in Journal of Personality and Social Psychology, 100(3), 387–405.
24. Developmental intergroup theory: Explaining and reducing children's social stereotyping and prejudice (2007) by Bigler, & Liben, in *Current Directions in Psychological Science, 16*(3), 162–166.
25. Oxytocin reactivity during intergroup conflict in wild chimpanzees (2016) by Samuni et al. In Anthroplogy Vol 114, N 2.
26. Zero-Sum Game Meaning: Examples of Zero-Sum Games - 2024 - MasterClass
27. Intimacy and Desire Peter Schnack

Enemy as a way of bonding *Published in final edited form as:*

Psychol Sci. 2011 Mar; 22(3): 10.1177/0956797610397667.

28. Us versus Them: Social Identity Shapes Neural Responses to Intergroup Competition and Harm

29. *The altruism question: Toward a social-psychological answer (1991) By Baston.*

30. The Social Neuroscience of Empathy (2009) Decety, J., & Ickes, W. (Eds.). in Boston Review.

31. Group Morality and Intergroup Relations: Cross-Cultural and Experimental Evidence. (2006). In Personality and Social Psychology Bulletin, 32, 1559-157

32. The powerful way that 'normalisation' shapes our world (bbc.com)

33. 40 Gig Economy Statistics You Must Learn: 2024 Market Share & Data Analysis - Financesonline.com

34. Rule Makers and Rule Breakers by M Gelfand Is Your Culture 'Tight' or 'Loose'? The Answer Could Explain Everything - The New York Times (nytimes.com)

35. Strategic Behavior with Tight, Loose, and Polarized Norms. (2024). Polarized cultures tend to individuals that act polarized and loose organizations, tend to have individuals with wide variance in their behaviors. https://pubsonline.informs.org/doi/abs/10.1287/mnsc.2023.01022?journalCode=mnsc

36. Organizational Culture-Performance Relationships: Views of Excellence and Theory Z. By Fred C. Lunenburg (2011) NATIONAL FORUM OF EDUCATIONAL

ADMINISTRATION AND SUPERVISION JOURNAL.
VOLUME 29, NUMBER 4, 2011.

37. Strategic Behavior with Tight, Loose and Polarized
    Norms. (2023). By Eugen Dimant, Michele J. Gelfand,
    Anna Hochleitner, Silvia Sonderegger. Standford
    Graduate School of Business. Working Paper No. 4125
    What Makes a Good Interaction Between Divided Groups?
    (berkeley.edu)

More Friendship As Medicine

38. "Overly Shallow? Miscalibrated Expectations Create a
    Barrier to Deeper Conversation," (2021) by Michael
    Kardas, PhD, Northwestern University; Amit Kumar, PhD,
    University of Texas at Austin; and Nicholas Epley, PhD,
    University of Chicago. "Journal of Personality and Social
    Psychology," published online Sept. 30, 2021.

39. An exploratory study of friendship characteristics and their
    relations with hedonic and eudaimonic well-being (2019)
    by Austen R. Anderson et al. Journal of Social and Personal
    Relationships Volume 37, Issue 1

40. Key Emotions of Friendships: love, attachment, trust,
    affinity, self-esteem (its emotional aspect), altruism,
    embarrassment and hope. Moreover, in a negative way,
    resentment, envy, susceptibility, jealousy and shyness.
    Could We Think About Friendship Relationships Without
    Emotions? The Other-Oriented Emotions (2018) by Ana
    Romero-Iribas and Consuelo Martínez-Priego

https://www.europeanproceedings.com/article/10.15405/epsbs.2019.01.2

41. https://rtc.london/making-friends/

42. https://www.apa.org/monitor/2023/06/cover-story-science-friendship

43. Adult friendship and wellbeing: A systematic review with practical implications (2023) by Christos Pezirkianidis, et al. . Front. Psychol., Sec. Positive Psychology, Volume 14

44. Platonic, How the Science of Attachment Can Help You Make--and Keep--Friends Hardcover (2022) Maria G Franco, Phd

45. Gottman's work on Trust and Commitment https://greatergood.berkeley.edu/article/item/john_gottman_on_trust_and_betrayal

46. Sophia Caron et al, How to Cancel Plans With Friends:

47. A Mixed Methods Study of Strategy and Experience (2023) by Sophia Caron, Collabra: Psychology (2023).

More Enlighted Loss

48. 330 Billion cells Turnover https://www.scientificamerican.com/article/our-bodies-replace-billions-of-cells-every-day/

49. The social readjustment rating scale (1967). Holmes TH, Rahe RH. *Journal of Psychosomatic Research*.

50. Marketing is based on our fear of loss: 10 Loss Aversion Marketing Tactics to Help Your Small Business Retain Customers and Win Sales - crowdspring Blog

51. Letting Go Of "Stuff" After a Loss - The Grief Recovery Method

52. Minimization & Unraveling the Mindset of Victimhood | Scientific American

53. https://www.ncbi.nlm.nih.gov/pmc/articles/PMC7700553/ #B7-behavsci-10-00177

Conclusion

54. What Is Social Capital? A Comprehensive Review of the Concept (2009) inAsian Journal of Social Science 37(3):480-510

55. Mind the Gap: Hierarchies, Health, and Human Evolution Hardcover (2001) by R Wilkinson (

56. What Really Made Primate Brains So Big? | Smithsonian (smithsonianmag.com)

https://www.smithsonianmag.com/science-nature/what-really-made-primate-brains-so-big-180962717/

57. Dunbar's number: Why we can only maintain 150 relationships (bbc.com)

https://www.bbc.com/future/article/20191001-dunbars-number-why-we-can-only-maintain-150-relationships

Dunbar, R.I.M. (1992a). Neocortex size as a constraint on group size in primates. Journal of Human Evolution 20: 469-493.

58. Living through war: Mental health of children and youth in conflict-affected areas | International Review of the Red Cross (icrc.org)

59. Podcast: The Menstrual Cycle, Stigma, and Mental Health (psychcentral.com)

60. Causal Relationships between the Psychological Acceptance Process of Athletic Injury and Athletic Rehabilitation Behavior - PMC (nih.gov)

61. Social belonging: brain structure and function is linked to membership in sports teams, religious groups, and social clubs - PMC (nih.gov)

62. Behave (2017). Robert Sapolsky. Penguin Press.

FACTS

or

OPINIONS

A MINDFUL DISCIPLINE

to choose your truth

Identify the facts from opinions in a recent interaction

WHAT I NOTICED

WHAT I THOUGHT ABOUT WHAT I NOTICED

Something that is true and can be proven with observable evidence.

Cannot be proven because it is based on personal feelings or preferences

HanDOUTS

The British Statistician George Box once quipped: "All models are wrong, some are useful." The following pages include models designed and depicted by Krystal using diverse education, training and experience in psychology, leadership, group dynamics, social engagement and community development. Use them, interpret them or disregard them using your own inner compass and group intentions to shape your selection. Should you desire a deeper dive, fuller explanation, diverse conversation or collaboration or suggested applications for these models, please reach out on social media or to krystal@theexecutiveshaman.com.

Simply, these handouts are one way we can/your group can start, continue or dive deeper into a more effective collaborative process.

Real

Is the idea genuine? Does it represent the truth, and comes from a place of authentic intention? Is the idea what the person really wants, or is it a substitution for or a deflection away from what is real?

Necessary

Does the idea/task/work meet or fill a need for the target audience? What would happen if you didn't do the work?

Meaningful

Does the idea speak to the heart? Does it feel good? Does it bring joy, satisfaction and fulfillment either to those who are doing the work, or receiving the benefits of the work?

Clever

Is the idea based on a business opportunity? It is based on informed evidence & research? Is the idea innovative, or out of the box, or unusual in some way?

Achieveable

Do the people that are going to be following through with the work of the idea have the capacity, the band-with, the resources and the guts to follow through with the work RIGHT NOW?

FIVE QUALITIES REQUIRED THAT MAK
A "Good" Idea

THE NEXT TIME YOU GIVE GUIDANCE, CONSIDER HOW MANY OF THE 5 QUALITIES YOUR OFFERED ADVICE INCORPORATES.

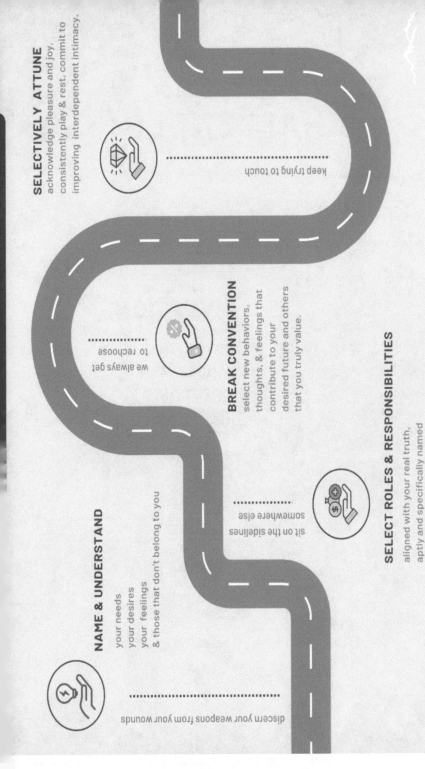

SELECTIVELY ATTUNE

acknowledge pleasure and joy,
consistently play & rest, commit to
improving interdependent intimacy.

keep trying to touch

BREAK CONVENTION

select new behaviors,
thoughts, & feelings that
contribute to your
desired future and others
that you truly value.

we always get
to rechoose

SELECT ROLES & RESPONSIBILITIES

aligned with your real truth,
aptly and specifically named
and in service to conscious
connection

sit on the sidelines
somewhere else

NAME & UNDERSTAND

your needs
your desires
your feelings
& those that don't belong to you

discern your weapons from your wounds

DR KRYSTAL WHIT
LEADERSHIP PSYCHOLOGIST

DIFFERENT FORMS OF
CHALLENGES

DIVERSIONS
WHO OR WHAT
CHANGES YOUR
DIRECTION?

PUSH BACKS
WHO OR WHAT
CONSTRAINS YOU?

OBSTACLES
WHO OR WHAT GETS IN
YOUR WAY?

ADVANCERS
WHO OR WHAT
PROPELS YOU?

4 TYPES OF GROWTH

Recognizing how you are growing will improve your motivation to endure the growth process. Reinforcing, or adding intentional support, to a specific type of growth, is likely to improve the efficacy of any growth effort.

ENLIGHTENMENT

Enlightenment occurs when something is recognized, understood, clarified, or integrated. This type of growth focuses UPWARD. It requires an investment of presence, a willingness to receive, truthfulness, agility, & vulnerability.

HEALING

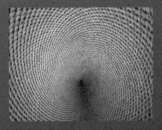

Healing occurs when something is restored, repaired, cured, completed or made whole. This type of growth focuses INWARD. It requires an investment of slowness, compassion, retreating from normal operations, ensuring safe environments & interactions, trust in the process.

EXPANSION

Expansion occurs when something is proliferated, replicated or increased. This type of growth focuses OUTWARD. It requires an investment of expression, power, resources, & wise choices regarding timing & context.

PROGRESS

Progress happens as something is advances or develops. This type of growth focuses ONWARD. It requires an investment of intention, courage to address resistance, cultivating learning environments & innovative relationships, & attention to skill improvement.

DR KRYSTAL WHITE
LEADERSHIP PSYCHOLOGIST

UNCONVENTIONAL TOLERANCE LIMITS

PLEASURE

Describe your limit to feeling joyful, experiencing easy success, taking it easy or fostering comfort & pleasure

PAIN

Describe your limit to endure conflict, feel discomfort, deal with hurt & tackle tough challenges

UNCERTAINTY

Describe your limit to "not knowing," confusion, being disconnected, leaving things open, taking space, "gray areas," letting go, risk, trusting others

CHANGE

Describe your limit to switching plans, redefining commitments, altering decisions, shifting values, & priorities, changing strategies, seeking new resources and altering traditions.

DR KRYSTAL WHITE
LEADERSHIP PSYCHOLOGIST

ROLES WE PLAY
WHEN SOMEONE REJECTS US

DR KRYSTAL WHITE

1 THE PUFFER FISH
EXPLODE, LASH OUT, BURN BRIDGES IMPLODE, SILENT TREATMENT, SELF-SABOTAGE

2 THE COOL KID
FEIGN INDIFFERENCE, BRUSH IT OFF. APATHY, MAKE JOKES, PRETEND YOU DIDN'T WANT IN THE 1st PLACE

3 THE CRITIC
NITPICK, FAULT FIND , SCRUNTIZE, RUMINATE OVER THE LOGIC, THE PROCESS OR WHY IT OCCURED, TOWARDS SELF OR OTHER

4 THE REBOUNDER
MOVE ON TO SOMETHING/SOMEONE ELSE QUICKLY, DO NOT TAKE TIME RO RECOVER, FOCUS ON WORK IN LESS SOCIALLY RISKY AREAS.

5 THE DENIER
PRETEND IT DIDN'T HAPPEN, CHANGE ASPECTS OF REALITY TO REDUCE VULNERABILITY, SPREAD REJECTION ONTO SOMEONE OR SOMETHING ELSE.

+IDENTIFY POSITIVE EXPRESSIONS FOR EACH

-IDENTIFY NEGATIVE EXPRESSIONS FOR EACH

EVOLUTION MODEL

WHAT % OF YOUR FOCUS IS SPENT IN EACH?

WHAT IS THE IMPACT?

FROM A PERSONAL STRESS FOCUS

TO A SOCIAL SUCCESS FOCUS

COPE

ADAPT

LEAD

CHECK IN

Step 1. Determine your intention.

Step 2. Select a question that best supports this intention.

Step 3. Inform the group of how the tool works. How you introduce, explain and facilitate Check In reflects your style, brand and mood. Make sure that you include the guidelines.

Step 4. Share the Check In question.

Step 5. Ask for a volunteer to go first.

Step 6. Step in when there is someone who doesn't follow the guidelines.

Step 7. Debrief the group with your intention in mind.

Extra credit: Ask one person in the group to give you feedback after the entire meeting is over.

"We're going to start our time with a process called Check In. This method helps teams be more present, engaged and synchronized. It is a structured way we can express ourselves and to listen to each other. Here is how it works:

The leader selects a question

Everyone here answers the question. There is no right way or wrong way to answer. How you interpret the question is up to you. How you answer is up to you.

When a person is answering, please just listen. Do not interrupt, do not ask questions, do not make comments. Just receive what that person wants to share.

After everyone has checked in, you can come back to something that was shared and discuss as a group

Someone volunteers to answer the question first.

When we each finish answering the question, we call on who we'd like to hear from next Any questions?"

Inter-dependence
COMPARISON CHART

DR KRYSTAL WHITE
LEADERSHIP-PSYCHOLOGIST
EXECUTIVE SHAMAN

SUPPORT

WE NEED SUPPORT.

WHEN RECEIVED, SUPPORT ALLOWS US TO FUNCTION <u>ADEQUATELY.</u>

VS

HELP

WE WANT HELP.

WHEN RECEIVED, HELP ALLOWS US TO FUNCTION <u>BETTER.</u>

WHICH ONE DO YOU HAVE MORE OF A CHALLENGE ASKING FOR OR ACCEPTING FROM OTHERS?

Affirmation Pages

The following pages contain affirmations that were socially curated, with the intention of uplifting, guiding and inspiring others in our communities. Many of the affirmations you see here were created during Free Leadership Workshops, and our community events. For example:

> **"Love is the question.
> When we really answer it, that's when the magic happens."**

At least a third of the affirmations here were generated during the May 18th 2024 book launchish event. Read more about that event in the Acknowledgements section.

COLLECTIVE AFFIRMATIONS
Unconventional Communities use collective affirmations as "prayers" for our shared future. Cut, Rip or Clip Out these collected affirmations. Use or Gift liberally.

Offer the medicine you've always needed

Ask the question that disrupts disillusion.

You have agency to craft our community

Accept you are loved, AS IS.

Raise Your Pleasure Tolerance

What if nothing was wrong?

Be More Sincere, Less Serious

JOY

Listen to your
Learn your
Love your
Live your

Move on.
Your past is not your potential

Let go of the feeling

Ensure that Sweetness is a sacred, staple of today.

You are not bound to the good intentions of others

Bask In the desires that are your birth right

Do the thing you can not not do

Complete the Necessary

Own Only What Truly Belongs to You

Trust the Process

Own Only What Truly Belongs to You

Remember your point

Create For Fun

Make Space cushions

We have the time to help it happen

Be the place where life comes more alive

The Universe invites you to Re-Choose

It's time to Tweak your Temple

Nothing that is meant for me will ever pass me by

How does it support you? ...& yes, it does!

Step Up Step Back or Stay which one serves our wellbeing today?

Be Patient for Answers

The Universe invites you to Re-Choose

Be a Bearer of
BRIGHTER NEWS

The World
needs more from us

MEDICINE
FRIENDSHIP IS

YOU DON'T HAVE TO BE THE
Boss
TO BE A LEADER

YOU'RE WHERE
you need to be

complete
the
necessary ✓

Express
with Kindness

Love
More

OVER FEAR

be your own player.
not a
spectator

love

what you attempt to

the past is not our
POTENTIAL

CHAPTER 11

ABOUT US

Here will be a genuine, heartfelt description of the people who supported this book's creation, who collaborated together, and who celebrated it's aims, themes and being-ness.

WELCOME.

"I really wanted a place where anyone felt

Lori Bishop
Owner, Blush Tea & Coffee,
answering the Check In:
"Why do you do what you do?"

A DIVERSE
COLLECTION OF
HUMANS
CONNECTED
TOGETHER

on May 18th, 2024.
They believed the
purpose was to
celebrate one person's
book. The real point
was to re-create and
celebrate community.
Some evidence is
collected here...

Make your move, Universe

WE WILL MAKE OURS.

DR KRYSTAL WHITE
LEADERSHIP PSYCHOLOGIST

ACKNOWLEDGEMENTS

I've said it before, and I'll need to keep saying it: I'm a pain in the ass to live with when I'm writing and completing a book. This is the 5th go around for me, and still the process reveals how much personal work I've got left to do.

I literally pretended that I was a bug the last week of writing this book. This went on for more than 5 minutes. I found the regressed emotional maturity to be alarmingly relieving. There's something that takes my mind over at the end of this process. This time, I obsessed about social dynamics and "the message" and "friendship is medicine" and Blah Blah Blah. Someone literally witnessed me bugging out. Another person (or three or four) listened to me whine about hiccups in the formatting process. A handful actually edited the chapters. A few contributed to the creative twists. A straight-shooter told me not to include "that part, this time." I socially bailed on numerous folks that I care about in order to prioritize this piece of meaningless purpose. ☺ Thank you for you all. There's no hierarchical order here. You all belong here. You all impact me.

Thank you, to you, who agreed that this book wasn't going to save the world, or the whales, or humanity, and yet also agreed that it was necessary work for me to devote my love and attention to.

Thank you, to those who are close to me, which may be the only reason you're reading this part. Listen—no matter what else happens, no matter what happened, or is happening NOW, the best role I'll ever play in life is that of a friend.

We do not know what we have almost done to ourselves— had we not chosen friendship. It's a choice many make, that I have made, for friendship is not for the faint-hearted. In a world that channels us to think in Black and White, thank you to all my friends who braved the journey to become one, for being present and available, for refusing to live locked into social expectation. Listen, the world I live in is deep, wide, and in technicolor. Friendship is the most defining, most challenging, and the most colorful thing I'll ever do. I am most humbled by, and I am most proud of my friendships. Those I didn't earn, and those I committed to when there was no rational benefit to them. The ones that broke up and broke me open, and the ones that saved my spirit when I least expected it.

I tell you this so that you know where I stand—I will continue to place it above all other goals, roles and flights of fancy.

Thank you to all those who said yes to Checking In and mindfully considering their answers to the questions I posed to them through the weaving of this book. I never know what I'm going to receive when I ask for your voice to step up, step in and share. How I've been delighted, shocked, sidelined, shaped, comforted and downright confused by the process of Check In. It's as if inside of us there are many small stones, buried for years or perhaps lifetimes. It's as if our Check Ins, our guided process of listening and sharing can stir them up, wrestle them from prolonged isolation, and touch the invisible. Without your willingness to answer big questions, this book would have been less cool.

To the wildly diverse, and consistently compassionate ownership of Grassroots Kava House—thank you for being a lighthouse. Your support at Free Leadership's inception provided space, mentoring, and spiritual start up fuel. I wasn't aware then that my heart craved more evidence and interaction with leaders like you all, in the neighborhood that I lived in. Thank you for your disciplined doing. Our collaboration is true, dynamic, and inspiring. Believe me, during the first year of founding the non-profit, there were many times I wanted to, and many hours that I did, give up. Your belief in me, in the mission of FLInc, and your practice in community service, hospitality, teamwork, artistry and FUN, matters.

That's what amazing, reciprocal and process-oriented partnerships do: they inspire you to keep believing when you've lost it for yourself. I am eager, willing, and energized to cheer for you all, check in for you, challenge you and celebrate you. Just call.

To all the bright spirits who gathered on May 18th to celebrate this book launchish—Isn't, everything in our world, shared? It is you all who keep me hopeful. It is me who grows wings in my spirit so that I can, maybe, lift us up from time to time. It is you who anchors me to a specific plot of land, so that I can, maybe, reign us in from time to time. It is rare to be in a space where people intentionally show up, are willing to open up, and ready to care without an ego needing someone to rescue.

Friendship is medicine, music is healing, and Blush Tea is welcoming.

A genuine "Thank You" for all those who were present with us, *and* for themselves. Most times, we arrive to social interactions with different intentions, diverse challenges, and divergent goals. Only by showing up we *can create* moments where we belong. Only by disciplined connection *can we leave* with more hope, and more capacity, for creating a future where such social wellbeing isn't rare anymore—it is the new status quo.

That's an unconventional community. And that was Us, on Saturday May 18th.

(Oh my goodness…I could copy and paste my acknowledgements from both Unconventional Citizens and Check In right here…because, the truth is: my past still matters. The rear-view mirror often motivates.

Is my life today worth all these wild words? We will only know if you ask me this question directly. I will Check In for you.)

Key: Thank you for reading the sign, for following your intuition. I hold holy trepidation for you. I acknowledge your attunement, your essential discernment, and your fight for slow, deliberate deep diving creation. It was you who reminded me of my center as I stitched this book together. It was your idea for the embedded QR codes and check ins. Your DNA is here, on this thing, right now.

Listening is your sacred mission. **Your** listening is a salve for the common ways society hurts, misunderstands and uses one another. And, you know: How easy is it for us all to hurt each other!!! How easy is it to marry our fears to our mindset!

Yet, our past is not our potential. Thank you for moving our attention to include more than just what hurts.

We've received the time, AND we will make space, for **what is really here for us**. Isn't it stones who serve as the womb of the universe's sounds? And stones, the instruments that carve vibrations from the earth, or maybe the air, itself? I do not know where prayers are born, nor where prayers flicker away to. I do know the sound of your open-heart, and "Of course, I've always known you…"

Maestro: Thank you for wanting more than breadcrumbs, and thank God, you aren't satisfied to scratch the surface. Just when I was self- secure enough to truthfully say "I attach securely," you got me to confess my insecurities. Just when I decided to avoid myself, you asked me to lunch. Just when I was boring myself, you got me to tap dance. If I am an avid player, you are an adept conductor. The instrument, the setting and the score, is irrelevant. There is a follower inside of us all, who is relieved to receive graceful guidance. Thank you, for reincarnating mine.

Boss: A lot of people who read my poetry book believe I was expressing real things about my real personal life.

I wonder if you believe that, too.

I wonder if you now believe the moon is Alien AI,[32] and I wonder if you're aware how far we've come.

I am committed to being truthful over being respectable—especially with you. Sometimes this dedication brings a whole lot of turmoil, especially to you. Yet--we have no further need to grieve our mistakes, our egos, our errors. We've met our quota, at least for this go around, don't you think? Thank you for <u>not staying the course</u> with me; thank you for making a new one together instead.

I mean it when I say: "Our connection is a radical invitation; we always get to rechoose." I choose to adore you. I choose to hold us both, and the world, to our best. I don't have to tell you that you are your own North Star, a bearer of brighter news. I'll remind you, however, when your conviction falters, of your power.

To Chris Ashbrook---You don't have to be the boss to be a Leader. Thank you for giving these words and letting me run with them for our vision at Free Leadership Inc. I am grateful and fueled by our shared commitment to integrity, emotional intelligence and competency in leadership.

---

[32] Another shameless reference to Unconventional Citizens, This is What Happens When My Ego Gets Hooked

To Chad Christian Cook--Love more over fear---that tagline originated from one of your answers during a very personal Check In, in March of 2024. I acknowledge how my insistence and esoteric waywardness unsettles the US, sometimes. Thank you for your gracious, truth-biting trust, tolerating the process.

To my clients and those I serve—you are the reason I must keep my own personal shit together. Thank you for influencing me, as much as I influence you.

To the one who named me Houdini—everyone knows, you don't really exist. Thank you for being my safe house.

The truth is: I am, and this is, simply another product of connectivity.

You, the one with me now and here, reading this. I acknowledge you, dear reader, and honor our connection.

There is an aliveness growing inside of us or it is surrounding us. I can't tell from where it emanates, nor where it goes. I can only tell you that it's asking that we dissolve the myth of self-sufficiency, that we breathe more consciously, that we tell tales of fervent friendships, and that we disinherit our arrogant aloofness.

Here is to the life we are willing to co-create together, the communities we are ready and willing to take responsibility for shifting, and for our world, who needs more from us.

Yes.

We are here for this.

And this (do you trust it yet?)

.... this is always for you.

We are worthy

We are ready

We are capable

We are wiling

To recreate, receive and relove a new land.

ABOUT

Krystal White, Ph.D., is a leadership psychologist with almost twenty five years of experience working as change agent and culture strategist, community engagement catalyzer, team performance expert, and holistic executive coach.

She specializes in optimizing group dynamics primarily in male dominated industries, and developing learning environments and programs designed to build prosocial skills. She continues to serve as an organizational culture consultant and leadership facilitator to social enterprises and mission oriented teams.

She is passionate about cultivating collaboration between diverse stakeholders, identifying and inspiring emerging leaders, and mobilizing seasoned leaders towards their legacy. Dr. White launched a non-profit in 2023 that generates civic engagement and social capital. It's vision is to find, proliferate and equip individuals to be better friends, mindful mentors and informal coaches.

Dr. White is a board-certified clinical psychologist and completed a medical fellowship at Madigan Army Medical Center in developmental psychology. She is military trained in the field of change leadership. She earned a Master's degree in Christian leadership from Fuller Theological Seminary, as well as a Master's degress in psychology, focusing on the integration of spirituality and psychology. She holds a master's degree in mind, brain, and education from Harvard University.

She has served as a radio personality, a podcaster, an educator, a group fitness instructor, a community mentor and a performance coach.

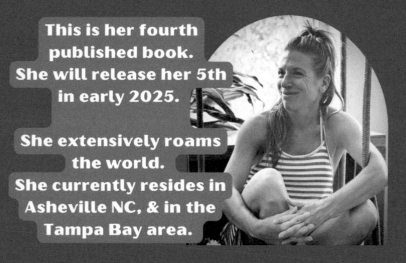

This is her fourth published book. She will release her 5th in early 2025.

She extensively roams the world. She currently resides in Asheville NC, & in the Tampa Bay area.

Create something
of your own here

this is
all
for
you

Made in the USA
Columbia, SC
01 December 2024

48098043R00180